METHODS OF THE MASTERS
Degas

METHODS OF THE MASTERS
Degas

TREWIN COPPLESTONE

Brian Trodd Publishing House Limited

Published in 1990 by
Brian Trodd Publishing House Limited
27 Swinton Street, London WC1X 9NW

Copyright © 1990 Brian Trodd Publishing House Limited

ISBN 1 85361 098 4

Printed in Hong Kong

Contents

Degas' Life

Degas was the eldest of five children. His father was the Paris manager of the family bank which was owned by his grandfather. Degas' grandfather had lived in Naples since leaving France at the time of the Revolution of 1789, having had the tragic and traumatic experience of witnessing the execution in the Place de la Concorde of his fiancée Hélène Vatrin. His lack of sympathy with the Revolution and a warning of personal danger led to his fleeing Paris in 1793. Degas' mother, Célestine Musson, was of Creole origin from New Orleans. The Creoles of Louisiana were French, Spanish or Portuguese descendants of settlers who retained their own patois and culture. Degas remained, despite wide travel and an important visit to New Orleans, essentially a Parisian with a strong sense of his own privileged position in society and the responsibility which he carried as the eldest son – a responsibility which was to have important and damaging consequences later in his life.

Although always associated in the public mind with Impressionism, Degas was in many ways a figure apart, closer socially to Manet than to any of the other Impressionists. Even his friendship with Manet was on the cool, reserved side; at one time an injudicious act by Manet caused a rift between them for a while. Degas participated in all but two of the eight Impressionist exhibitions and at least to this extent he must be included in the Impressionist movement.

His education and background were against the likelihood of his becoming a revolutionary independent in whatever career he chose to adopt. That he should choose to be a painter was naturally unexpected and unwelcome to his father. In 1845 he entered the Lycée Louis le Grand as a boarder and received a strict and standard classical education, learning Greek, Latin and some German. He also acquired a love of the French classics which became so much a lifelong passion that it infused his whole nature and is evident in his art. His classical training became part of the foundation of his intellectual character and was allied to what was an essentially exploratory, experimental spirit. Although he presented a cool, aloof exterior to the world he was imbued with a restless curiosity which he indulged in private.

While at school he met as his contemporaries a number of boys who remained his friends for the remainder of his or their lives – notably Henri Rouart and Paul Valpinçon.

Degas acquired an early taste for art and was fortunate that his father was also keen on the arts. To accommodate his father's wishes (his enthusiasm for art did not extend to any wish to see his son embark on such a precarious and socially inappropriate career), he entered law school in 1853, but he spent his time drawing and visiting the studios of artists, particularly that of an undistinguished painter, Barrias. He also spent much time in the Louvre and viewing a number of private collections owned by friends of his father. The works he saw confirmed his intellectual predilection for classical order. At this time too, he enrolled in the Print Room of the Bibliothèque Nationale where he made copies of Renaissance works by Mantegna, Raphael and Dürer.

One of the private collections that he much enjoyed was that of the father of his friend Paul

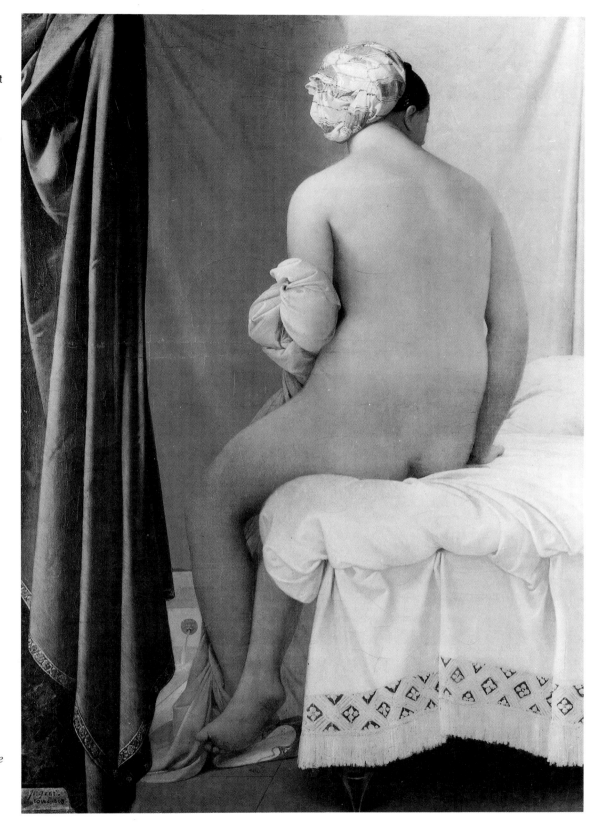

Left: *Self Portrait*
*c.*1857–58   Oil on paper
mounted on canvas
26 × 19 cm (10¼ × 7½ in)
Sterling and Francine Clark Art
Institute, Williamstown,
Massachusetts
*As a young man of 23 Degas
is already showing a
distinction of drawing, control
of tone and sensitivity of
colour in this revealing
portrait. Something of his
privileged background and
sense of personal importance
comes through.*

Right: Jean Auguste
Dominique Ingres
Nude Bather
1808   Oil on canvas
146 × 97.5 cm (57½ × 38⅜ in)
Musée du Louvre, Paris
*This painting is often known
as the Valpinçon Bather since
it was once in the Valpinçon
Collection and was seen there
by Degas as a young man. The
delicacy and sensitivity of the
painting of the back reveals
Ingres' distinction as a great
draughtsman.*

Valpinçon. It was here that he first saw some of Ingres' finest works (including the important *Nude Bather* now in the Louvre). Through Valpinçon he met Ingres who, at one meeting, told him to 'draw lines, young man, many lines – from nature or from memory'. Whether influenced by this injunction or not, the sensitivity of Degas' line – in painting, pastel and watercolour as well as in drawing – is so highly distinguished that he is recognized as one of the truly great draughtsmen, a worthy successor to Ingres.

Degas never met Ingres' great contemporary, Delacroix, but he was influenced by him. Although he regarded, with some justice, Delacroix's drawing as coarse, he responded to the spirit of his Romantic work and this is evident in Degas' later work.

After a short period in Barrias' studio, at the

age of 21 he entered the studio of Louis Lamothe, a follower of Ingres who had recommended him. He also studied at the Ecole des Beaux-Arts where he met other young painters including Léon Bonnat and Fantin Latour both of whom became well known Independents.

At this time he made his first visit to Naples to meet his grandfather, and soon after again visited Italy (Naples and Rome) and southern France. He spent most of 1857 in Rome where he met other figures who had considerable influence on him. His continuing deep interest in music was encouraged by a meeting with Bizet, but the most important influence on his work was Gustave Moreau, whom he met in Rome but who lived and worked in Paris. He was to become something of an artistic father figure to the young Degas. Moreau's Romantic symbolism expressed a literary mythology with great intelligence in dense, highly personal imagery, and he directed Degas' attention to Delacroix and the great Renaissance Venetians, especially Titian. Moreau

was also a pastellist and his brilliant colour had much influence on Degas.

While in Italy Degas reinforced through study his interest in the classical and copied the work of the Renaissance masters, Michelangelo, Masaccio, Titian and particularly Leonardo, whose intellectual curiosity and experimental approach were much in sympathy with Degas' own.

In 1858 he visited Florence and stayed with the Bellelli family (the Baron's wife was Degas' aunt, his father's sister). He made numerous studies of the family while on this visit which resulted, on his return to Paris, in his first major portrait study in oils, *The Bellelli Family*. One of the studies for this painting is the first pastel considered in some detail in this book. The fact that the painting was completed in Paris is revealing about the method Degas adopted through his working life. His practice was to make studies of the elements of the work to be produced, to plan its composition, to make sketches of possible variants and then, when confirmed in his intention, to paint the finished work in his studio, usually without models, using only his preliminary sketches and plans. These studies and sketches were done in pencil, pastel, essence, monotype or oils and ranged from rough sketches of details to highly finished studies of individual elements.

It was also at this time, about 1860, that Degas' earliest classical subjects were painted. He also began to use pastels not only for sketches but for finished exhibition work. Although Degas was not unique in using pastel, it eventually became a method that he explored as few have done, and led to his becoming perhaps the greatest of all users of the medium.

New influences also intruded. He made his first acquaintance with Japanese art which had considerable influence on his compositional methods. Photography, then becoming popular, was a great interest and this, too, both influenced his compositional approach and provided him with valuable visual information. He met Manet, then the somewhat unwilling leader of an anti-academic group who met at the Café Guerbois. Although they were never close friends they came from a

Manet at Longchamps
c.1864   Pencil on buff paper
32 × 24.4 cm (12⅝ × 9⅝ in)
Metropolitan Museum of Art,
New York. Rogers Fund, 1918
An example of Degas' ability to capture the immediacy of a changing pose, and, having identified it, to fix the forms in convincing drawing. Note how the leg is changed in the final structure.

8

similar social background and had much in common. Manet, for instance, was the only other artist in the group to use horse racing as a subject — and probably even to visit the racecourse (one can hardly imagine Monet or Renoir at the races, and certainly not in the paddock or enclosure). There is a drawing by Degas of Manet at Longchamps. During a visit to the Valpinçons, Degas did the first drawings of racehorses, a subject that he treated extensively after 1866. One of the splendid examples of his horse and jockey works is the pastel *Jockeys in the Rain.*

At this time the essential public platform was the annual salon in Paris. It had become the major artistic social event of the year. Following the Revolution the Salon had been held at irregular intervals but from 1833 it had become the annual event it remained for the rest of the intervening period. It was organized through the government and held in the Grand Salon of the Louvre (hence its name). The choice of works to be included was determined by the Académie des Beaux-Arts which ensured that the avant garde, unorthodox or independent artists were excluded. This led to the organization of an Association of Artists with the

Above: Edouard Manet. *Le déjeuner sur l'herbe*
1863   Oil on canvas
214 × 270cm (84¼ × 106¼ in)
Musée d'Orsay, Paris
A familiar subject in France, the fête champêtre *traditionally presented an idealized romantic vision of the scene of a country picnic or party, the privileged indulging in mythological games as gods and goddesses. This down-to-earth version, with its sexual overtones, was too much for the prevailing taste, held to be indecent and critically condemned.*

Overleaf: *Misfortunes of the City of Orléans in the Middle Ages*
1865   Oil on canvas
85 × 147 cm (33½ × 57⅞ in)
Musée d'Orsay, Paris
Degas was soon to abandon the traditional historical allegory and this painting shows that however intellectually constructed and well painted in its details, it does not combine effectively as a composition. This suggests that Degas was less interested in the story than in the drawing of the individual figures and the horses.

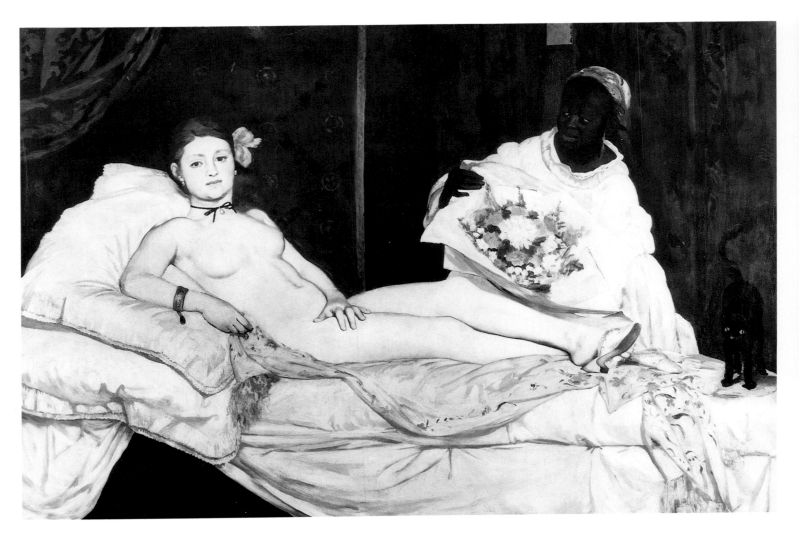

intention of holding an independent salon. Its 3,000 members included Delacroix, Daumier and the Barbizon painter, Théodore Rousseau. Although this independent salon was never held it was, in idea, a precursor of the independent exhibitions of the later years of the century, and it identified discontent with the academic authoritarianism of the Académie and the Salon.

By the 1860s the Salon had become firmly entrenched as both the only place in which public recognition could easily be obtained and an exclusion zone for the majority of young creative spirits. The scandal of the 1863 Salon which rejected many of the finest non-academic painters resulted in the holding of the Salon des Refusés, suggested (ordered?) by Napoleon III ostensibly to establish the superiority of the Salon artists over the rejected artists. Among the rejected was Manet's *Le déjeuner sur l'herbe*, a modern interpretation of a Renaissance composition by Raphael which had been engraved by MarcAntonio Raimondi and was available in Paris. The painting caused a scandal, was held to be obscene, and the exhibition was closed early. Manet, as a result, became an unwilling focus for all dissident opposition to the academic hierarchy.

Degas did not submit to this Salon but in 1865

he exhibited his historical allegory *Misfortunes of the City of Orléans in the Middle Ages (Malheurs de la ville d'Orléans)*. In this year Manet received even wider notoriety with his painting *Olympia* since it was also exhibited in the Salon. *Olympia* was a modern reclining nude following the Renaissance model of Giorgione and Titian. Manet's painting was, however, distinctly unlike the traditional nude. Paul Valéry's comments in his short study of Manet perhaps best indicate the causes of offence that the painting created. He describes the subject of the work as 'the cold and naked Olympia, a monster of commonplace sensuality, ministered by a negress'. He also observes that her empty head is separated from her 'essential being' by a small black velvet band. 'Impurity personified' he calls her, identifying her as a prostitute.

Manet spent much time in conversation with his avant garde friends, writers and artists at the Café Guerbois. Among these was Degas whose position at this time was similar to Manet's. He was sometimes accepted at the Salon but more often rejected; after 1870 he submitted no more paintings to the Salon. The Café Guerbois played an important part in the development of Impressionism, acting as its theoretical forcing

Above left: Edouard Manet.
Olympia
1865   Oil on canvas
130 × 190 cm (51$\frac{1}{5}$ × 74$\frac{4}{5}$ in)
Musée d'Orsay, Paris

Above: *The Wounded Jockey*
1866   Oil on canvas
180.4 × 151 cm (71 × 59$\frac{1}{2}$ in)
Collection of Mr and Mrs Paul
Mellon, Upperville, Virginia

While the painting shows a lively interest in the action of the horses it still reveals the traditional understanding of the spreadeagled legs which Muybridge disproved. The suggestion of the jockey having fallen from the riderless horse is practically not feasible — he must have fallen from an earlier horse.

house. Here Degas met Pissarro, Renoir, Monet and Sisley, the essential creative figures of the movement. He also met Cézanne and Zola and the theorist of the group, Edmond Duranty, author of *La Nouvelle Peinture* and *Réalisme*. Duranty believed that artists should show 'the social side of man'. He also included Degas by name in one of his novels and became his close friend. Degas painted a magnificent pastel of Duranty which is illustrated and examined here (page 58).

During the 1860s Degas expanded the range of his subject matter, abandoning historical painting in 1866. In the same year he exhibited at the Salon *The Wounded Jockey*, the first painting to show his new interest in horses, jockeys and horse racing, an interest which lasted until the late 1870s. He also undertook some portraits, mainly of his family and friends, not on commission. Other subjects were the musicians of the orchestra at the Opera and a short series of landscapes which were usually not painted in the open air but recollected in tranquillity in his studio. Most of these were in pastel.

The Franco–Prussian War of 1870 caused a dramatic disruption to the cultural life of Paris and led to a general dispersal of writers and artists in response to the war. Of the Impressionists to be, Pissarro and Monet went to London, Sisley to Belgium, Renoir was called up for military service, and Cézanne went to the south of France. Typically, Degas and Manet joined the National Guard and were involved in the siege of Paris. Manet was under the command of the painter Meissonier, an academic whose famous painting of Napoleon's retreat from Moscow was widely admired. Degas saw action in a gun battery which included, to his great pleasure, two of his boyhood friends, Paul Valpinçon and, as Commander of the battery, Henri Rouart. As a result of exposure in cold weather in the gun emplacements, Degas began to suffer from eye trouble which continued to worsen his sight for the rest of his life. From this time on he complained about his eyes although in the early years they were probably not as badly affected as he claimed. Nevertheless his eyesight steadily deteriorated. During the Commune which succeeded the siege he fortunately went to stay with the Valpinçons in the country, thus avoiding the riots which, as a member of the National Guard, might have cost him his life.

In 1872 he visited New Orleans with his brother René who was, with another brother Achille, a cotton merchant there. Degas stayed about six months and made many studies and paintings of

Cotton Merchants at Market:
The Cotton Exchange at
New Orleans
1873   Oil on canvas
74 × 92 cm (29¹/₅ × 36¹/₄ in)
Musée d'Orsay, Paris
One of the earliest of Degas'
paintings to reveal his
compositional ingenuity and
inventiveness. The drawing
is authoritative and keenly
observing of the active
commercial scene.

the family and friends. Also while there he made studies for his important painting *Cotton Merchants at Market: The Cotton Exchange (Bureau de coton à la Nouvelle-Orléans)*. He painted the finished work on his return to Paris.

Before the visit he had begun to go to the Opera House of the Rue le Peletier, and on returning from New Orleans this interest expanded to give him the subject matter for his best known works — his paintings of theatre and especially ballet.

In 1873 his father became seriously ill in Naples and in February 1874 he died. This revealed a serious financial situation which was to affect Degas' whole life. When Degas appealed to his brother René for help in clearing the debts it emerged that he, too, had financial problems and was going to need help himself. Degas, characteristically, as the eldest son, assumed responsibility and sold most of his valuable collection of paintings, including important pastels by Quentin de la Tour. From this time forward Degas, who had been something of a dilettante, not depending exclusively on his painting for an income, became a professional artist with the need to sell work to live. For Degas this was an uncomfortable and at times depressing experience. His consciousness of his social status caused him some embarrassment in his dealings with customers for his paintings. Perhaps it is also interesting and appropriate to note here that his relationship with even his friends over his work was not always easy and at times could become acrimonious. As a perfectionist, whenever Degas saw one of his paintings at a friend's house or even in a gallery, he wished to alter it, 'improve it'. From experience, his friends learned to resist the suggestion, since if he once removed a painting they had great difficulty in repossessing it. Hence the acrimony. One painting that Rouart was finally persuaded to part with never resurfaced. It must be admitted that some time later Degas reluctantly sent him another.

It should be remembered that at this time the system of dealers and agents had not become a familiar part of the art scene. Apart from the Salon and some other officially organized exhibitions, the only opportunity of showing work to the public was to find a private room or to show in one's own studio and to undertake all advertising oneself. Some shops dealing in artists' materials had already begun to show work on their premises but this did not amount to a properly organized system.

Below: *Dancer Putting on her Stocking*
c.1900 Bronze
47 cm high (18½ in)
Tate Gallery, London
In his later years Degas' failing eyesight caused him considerable distress and difficulty and the tactile opportunities offered by sculpture proved a great boon to him. He made studies in most of his popular themes including dancers, women bathing and some particularly vivid studies of horses in action.

Left: *Mme. Lala at the Cirque Fernando*
1879   Pastel
61 × 47.7 cm (24 × 18¾ in)
Tate Gallery, London

Of course the young painters — then as now — expected difficulty in gaining recognition and it was only the evident abilities of such painters as Manet, Monet and Degas that attracted a number of sensitive, cultured people — writers, artists and savants — into opening galleries and inviting painters to exhibit.

Despite Degas' financial difficulties, which engaged much of his time, he was one of the prime movers in organizing the first Impressionist exhibition which took place in the same year that his father died (1874) at the former studio of a well known Parisian photographer, Nadar, at 35 Boulevard des Capucines. The formal title of the show was *Première Exposition de la Société Anonyme des Artistes, Peintres, Sculpteurs, Graveurs*. It was the first of eight shows, none of which was officially known as an Impressionist exhibition.

When Degas returned from New Orleans he moved to 17 Rue Blanche and found that his friends had transferred their allegiance from the Café Guerbois to the Nouvelle Athènes. There he met George Moore, the perceptive Irish writer, whose observations on painting are a valuable source of information on the painters and their work.

The second Impressionist exhibition took place in 1876, the third in 1877, the fourth in 1879, and thereafter they were held annually until 1882 with the eighth and last in 1886. Although the participating artists were subjected to venomous criticism for the early exhibitions, by the time of the last the artistic atmosphere had changed and most of the Impressionists had become successful. Degas, working privately, almost reclusively, was successful through the whole period and as his work progressed he incorporated all the subjects for which he is well known. In 1879 *The Cotton Exchange* was bought by the Pau Museum, becoming his first work to hang in a public museum.

Degas' own view of the Impressionist exhibitions was that they should present a wide conspectus of 'independent', not exclusively Impressionist, work — whatever that actually was. He wanted the shows to be called the 'Independents' and eventually convinced the group that the word should be incorporated in the title. He also expressed his belief in the need for a Salon of Realists. He was then full of confidence and energy but his views did not prevail and the shows continued to be predominantly Impressionist in character. Although other painters now unknown — except perhaps to specialist historians — participated in the shows, it was the work of Monet, Renoir and the others that set the character of the shows and constituted the majority of the paintings to be seen. It is, incidentally, in keeping with Manet's character that he refused to exhibit despite his earlier role.

Through the late 1870s and early 1880s Degas continued his studies of dance and horse subjects but he also embarked on a series of paintings which may be described as social subjects: laundresses, milliners' shops, café scenes, pedestrians, and the girls who were walking the streets. Increasingly, however, it was the dance that attracted him, and pastel painting drew him as a method of capturing both the solid forms of the dancers and the transient, delicate, light effects of the dance itself.

In the mid-1880s he began to explore his last new range of subject matter — the presentation of women in the intimacy of their bathroom, engaged in their toilette, bathing, combing their hair, etc. Unselfconscious, supposing themselves to be unobserved, they do not pose or try to present themselves for public approval; but awkwardly, sometimes contorting themselves to dry their bodies, their essential physical nature is shown with a sympathy and understanding that awakens compassion and affection in the viewer. *Olympia* and Manet's clear and uncompromising objective study is a far cry from these works.

As mentioned earlier, Degas' eyesight began to deteriorate after 1870, and throughout the 1880s there was a gradual weakening to the extent that in 1892 he was virtually obliged to give up oil painting. From this time his usual method of working was with pastel, sometimes in combination with a monotype under-image. As a result of his very poor eyesight his colours became bolder and his drawing less refined. However his habit of making many studies and then drawing largely from memory and imagination enabled him to continue painting and produce some extremely powerful work.

It was not, in fact, until 1893 that he held his first one-man exhibition at Durand Ruel's gallery. Durand Ruel was one of the new breed of patron dealers and was a particular supporter of the Impressionists. Degas showed mainly — and perhaps surprisingly — landscapes in pastel and monotype.

The last great phase of his work, and one of the most admired, consists mainly of studies of women, which had been the subject of most of his works in the last Impressionist show, and some late studies of ballet dancers drawn almost entirely from memory but with some little help from photographs.

From now until his death Degas was constantly preoccupied with his health and his eyesight. The possibility even of pastel drawing in these years became problematical so that he could only work on a large scale. Another medium left to him was sculpture which he could only dimly see but the forms of which responded to his touch in the clay.

In 1898 Degas met his brother René again after an estrangement which had lasted for many years

and which had come about as a result of René's divorce from his blind wife Estelle. Degas had thought René's behaviour indefensible and had felt it more strongly perhaps because of her blindness.

While he did contribute to the large Centennial Exhibition in Paris in 1900 he was becoming increasingly reclusive and indifferent to public fame. The death of family members and close friends, particularly that of Henri Rouart in 1912, further distressed and isolated him.

At the same time his public reputation grew. His paintings fetched high prices at the sale of Rouart's collection, one of his paintings reaching the highest price at that time achieved for the work of a living painter. In 1914 the magnificent Comondo collection, which included some of Degas' finest paintings, was added to the Louvre. This acceptance signalled the victory of the Impressionists over the academics. It also confirmed Degas, whatever his own feelings or intentions, as an inextricable part, not only of Impressionism but of the significant avant garde.

He died on 27 September 1917, in the middle of a world war of which he was hardly aware, and was buried in the family vault in Montmartre Cemetery — a Parisian in death as in life. He has remained one of the most respected, admired and loved painters of a period which saw the beginning of the whole modern movement.

Pastel:
History and
Method

Artists have used soft chalks and other dry pieces of coloured material throughout history. Indeed, the earliest cave paintings were effectively the first pastels since pastel painting is the nearest possible method to the ideal of the application of pure colour to a surface so that it remains there, unchanging, unaffected by external or internal conditions. This ideal is essentially unattainable since the atmosphere carries agents, such as water, which will damage the surface and eventually cause deterioration. It is the good fortune of very dry conditions that have preserved the cave paintings to this day and this is why the paintings are now not freely to be seen. Further internal damage may be caused by the chemical interaction of the powder colour (pigment) placed on the surface although, again in the case of the cave paintings, this was largely avoided by the use of earth source colours which did not interact in this way. There is also a further element to be considered in respect of the cave paintings. When colour is applied to a surface there is a certain capillary action which

Cave painting. *Room of the Bison*
Magdalenian *c.*12000 B.C.
Earth colours on rock surface
Altamira, Spain
The vivid and lively drawings of animals by prehistoric man are among their most effective portrayals in art. The details of the method employed are not known with certainty, but in the direct application of colour mixed with water as the only medium, they are the ideal precursors of pastel painting.

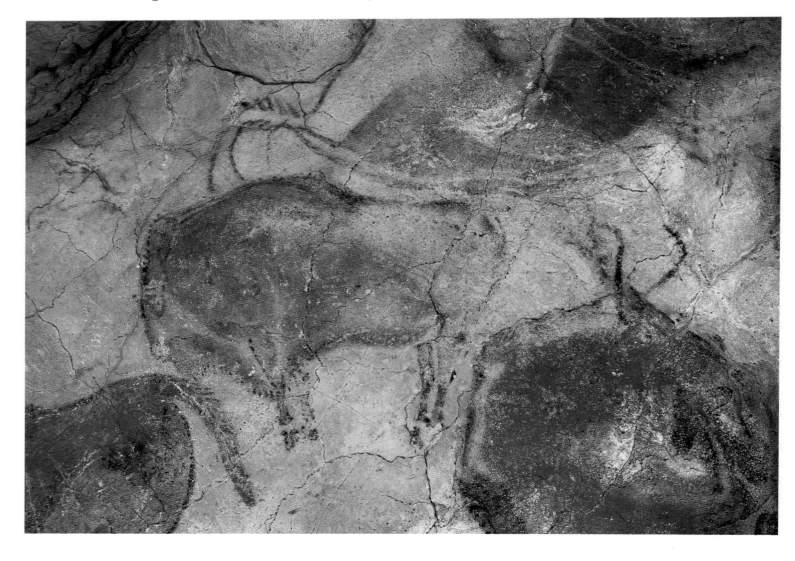

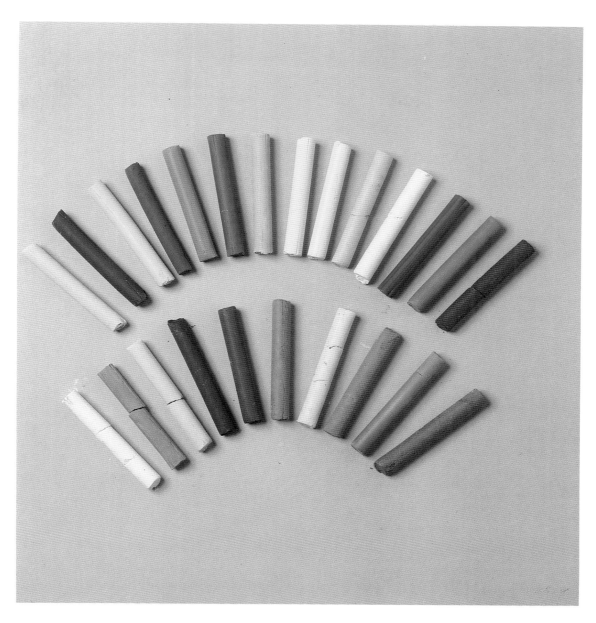

A display of pastel sticks. These are now available in degrees of hardness and softness to suit the individual.

temporarily tenuously attaches the colour, in this instance, to the rock face of the cave. As long as there is no movement in the surface holding the colour it is likely to stay attached and eventually to become incorporated into the surface, particularly if it is porous. Rock is uniquely appropriate for this process. Any other surface, exposed to the open atmosphere and subject to movement, such as a wall, a board or a piece of paper will lose its tenuous hold on the colour.

The practical problem of all painting, therefore, is to find a way of attaching colour to a surface with the minimum of colour adulteration and with maximum permanence. No method of doing this is perfect. Each of the developed methods has its advantages and disadvantages. The most permanent methods, such as oil paint, suffer the greatest deterioration of the colour, while those methods whose colours deteriorate least, are the least permanent, or perhaps might better be described as the most delicate. One such method is pastel.

In practical terms pastel is formed by mixing the pigment colour with a dry gum, gum tragacanth being the most popular and usual. When this mixture is manufactured in the form of a stick the standard modern pastel is achieved.

The colour range available in pastel is considerable. From the purest and most intense hue a range of tints and shades is obtainable from almost white to almost black. When the range of primaries, secondaries and tertiaries is treated in this way through adding white to arrive at tints and adding black to achieve shades it is evident that an enormous variation may be obtained. When it is also recognized that the method of colour application is simple and direct, and admits of surface mixing and overdrawing, the colour availability and subtlety become almost inexhaustible.

The greatest dangers arise from the delicacy of the attachment of pigment to the surface. Although not as insecure as pure pigment, the gum in pastel is only slightly more effective than pure colour until it is fixed – that is, fused to the surface. This process will be considered later.

21

Diagram. *This example of the linear use of pastel stick to provide both definition of area and, through cross or parallel hatching, linear surface effect indicates the textural versatility of the method.*

The method of pastel painting consists of drawing the pastel stick across the working surface so that the colour will be picked up by it. For this reason a slightly rough or uneven surface is usually desirable and is certainly that most frequently used.

Pastel colour has only surface colour, being an opaque, near-dry pigment. There is no 'glazing' effect; the superimposition of one colour over another, however thinly applied, does not result in show-through of the undercolour. Pastel colours do not yellow, turn brown, crack or change colour. Pastel colours, once applied, maintain their luminosity and hue and, as noted above, are available from the most intense to the palest. To this extent, and in many circumstances, pastel is a wonderfully effective and attractive method of picture making.

It has yet other attractions. Since it is a simple and direct method it responds to a great variety of different treatments and effects. It is effective in broad linear draughtsmanship and strong colour. It may be used to produce the most delicate and precisely drawn images of great tonal refinement. It may be used in conjunction with other methods to enhance or heighten an effect. It may, for instance, be used with watercolour (indeed it could itself be described as dry watercolour since, like watercolour, the pigment is bound with gum). It may also be used with a monotype base and it was a frequent practice of Degas' to use it in this way. It may even be used over oil paint or paintings done with essence (essential oils). Yet again, after the pastel has been applied directly with the stick, a brush, the fingers or a stump may be used to mix the colours into a solid tonal area rather than a linear effect on the surface. Yet again, a water-wet brush may be used on the applied pastel for special effects similar to gouache painting. Other explorations and combinations may be imagined. Since Degas was essentially an exploratory and innovative artist, pastel painting proved a great attraction to him throughout most of his life.

The above advantages having been noted it may be wondered why pastel has not proved more widely attractive to artists. There are two major disadvantages. The first, its susceptibility to damage, has already been noted. The second is that by its nature it does not lend itself to large-scale work. When one considers the difficulty of

Diagram. *A finger, a stump, cloth or some other absorbent material may be rubbed across the surface of a pastel to create a misty delicate effect which contrasts with linear overdrawing.*

Below right: Detail from *Jockeys Before the Race.* Essence on board, see page 69.
Degas used a variety of mixed media, including the use of 'essence'. This involves the mixture of pigment with an essential oil and gives the effect of a thin oil painting. The essential oils most used are oil of cloves, oil of lavender or spike oil.

protecting the finished work, any use of pastel for mural painting, for instance, seems unwise.

These things having been said, the pastel image is as permanent as any and more so than most.

For those readers who may be considering pastel painting, some practical observations may be helpful. Manufactured sticks can be delicate and brittle. Most writers on painting techniques recommend to artists that they manufacture their own pastel sticks. But the quality of modern pastel made by the reputable artists' materials' manufacturers is quite satisfactory. Those made in France are usually of high standard. There is perhaps one warning that should be given. Pastel sticks, of their nature, are somewhat messy in use and give rise to a quantity of dust. It is essential therefore that no pastels containing poisonous chemicals are used, such as emerald green, Naples yellow or chrome yellow, since the inhaling of the dust from these could be harmful. However, where such a colour is sold now under any of these names it will be a synthetic product, probably coal tar which, while innocuous, is not best in the pastel method.

The great range of colour is achieved, as

explained above, by the gradual and graded reduction of the most intense hues through the addition of increasing percentages of white or black pigment. Those whites include clay, alabaster, gypsum and zinc white. Talcum powder (French chalk) is also used which gives the slight 'soapiness' to the feel of the sticks and adds to their adhesive qualities. The different quality of covering power of the whites used is revealed dramatically when the pastel is fixed.

The support for a pastel painting may be paper, board or canvas and should have a medium surface texture. This quality is essential. Pastel does not work effectively on a smooth, impervious surface or on a very rough one, such as plaster or concrete. The surface to be used needs a certain tooth; with a smooth surface the colour will slide and will not be deposited, while with a very rough surface the stick will disintegrate. Most pastel users also find that a toned ground — grey, dull green or a dark brown for instance — proves the best in practice since the luminosity of the colour is enhanced by the deeper toned background and much of the colour in pastel is a tint. Degas always used a coloured paper or board for his pastels and occasionally this was of a strong colour into which he keyed his working colours.

Although the method is usually known as pastel

painting, in the use of a stick it seems more to resemble drawing. Since, however, using the stick like a pencil, linearly, is only part of the method and many different effects are achievable as indicated earlier, it is perhaps not entirely inappropriate to call the work painting. Many of Degas' pastels certainly give the impression of being painted.

Nevertheless most pastellists, including Degas, use line, cross-hatching, overdrawing, etc. to achieve the result they are seeking. Degas was a great draughtsman in the tradition of Raphael and Ingres and it was the linear quality of pastel that held some of its attraction for him. The possibilities in the use of the stick are not confined, of course, to purely linear working. The stick may be used along its length to produce toned areas and mixed on the surface to produce a rich variety of similar colour effects.

Mixed media effects may also be obtained as has been noted above. A watercolour base, sketching in the main blocks of forms in the painting, can be drawn over with pastel so that the watercolour underpainting shows through, giving a coherence to the composition. The freedom this gives in the use of the pastel enables the production of a denser image than with watercolour alone. It must be remembered that pastel is an opaque method and any overdrawing will entirely obscure the watercolour underpainting.

Left: Diagram. *Oil pastel sticks, perhaps not surprisingly, offer a less intense, more 'oily' colour effect. In this example the linear use is illustrated.*

Opposite: Diagram. *The use of charcoal in combination with pastel produces a richness of colour in direct sketching.*

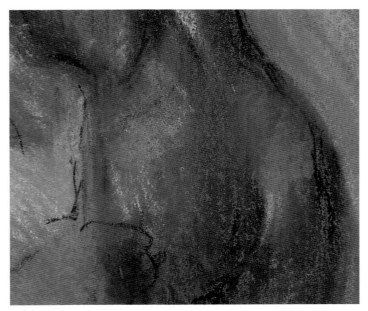

Left: Diagram. *A variety of textural effects achieved by the use of hard and soft pastels and stump and finger mixing. The achievement of atmospheric and light qualities is possible in this way.*

Above: Diagrams. *These two illustrations show the different effect of high and low key treatment in the use of pastel sticks. A richness of colour is achieved in each case.*

The use of monotype is similar to watercolour with one important difference, compositionally very significant. A monotype image is produced by painting on glass or another non-absorbent surface and, while the image is still wet, transferring it to a paper surface. The image on the paper is known as a monotype and is the reverse of the original. Usually only hand pressure is used to transfer the image and in consequence it is not very precise or even. However, the effect is often evocative and atmospheric. The reverse image provides a new compositional opportunity for pastel overdrawing. It was a method adopted frequently by Degas. It is worth remembering that the glass or other surface can be repainted with the original image since not all the colour is removed in the transfer. Each subsequent print is therefore similar but not identical and this gives further opportunity for experimentation with colour and composition.

Pastel pencils, more firmly bound with gum and glycerine than the standard pastel stick, are now available and although they do not have the qualities of true pastel they do have an attractive linear quality and are considerably less messy in use. They were not available in Degas' day.

Pastel sticks are manufactured now in varying degrees of hardness and softness. They may be mixed in use and experiment will reveal which type best suits the individual. Degas used soft pastels.

There is a further form of pastel, also not available to Degas, known as oil pastel, which may be used like oil paint. It does not mix easily with standard pastel although for certain effects there is no reason why they should not be combined. The sticks are bound in an oil and glycerine compound and do not, as a result, break as easily. But they are, of course, subject to more colour and physical change than standard pastel.

Throughout this consideration of the pastel method of painting its sensitive fragility over a long period of inevitable disturbance has been emphasized; it is therefore essential to give the surface some form of protection. Bearing in mind that any protective action that is taken which

rough thin impasto of the surface, or any covering of a binding fluid on the grains of colour diminishes to some degree the purity, freshness and 'sparkle' of the colour and flattens the quality of the thin impasto. Of course this is little evident when the whole pastel is covered since no comparison is possible but it is worth experimenting to the extent of 'fixing' one half of a pastel and allowing it to dry. The difference will then be apparent. Fixing must therefore be undertaken delicately, tentatively and slowly. Since in pastel the fine particles of colour lie irregularly and loosely over one another and reflect light from many different angles, it is important to restrict any movement or covering of the surface to the absolute minimum. The fixative, either blown through an oral spray or with an aerosol, should never be first applied straight onto the work but tested into space before lightly allowing a very fine mist to settle on the work. It is advisable to give the pastel a first fixing *in situ* where painted and later, but only if evidently necessary, an application when the work is flat. It will not be necessary to do more than hold the work vertically and give the edge a slight tap to discover whether it is sufficiently fixed — but even this must not be attempted with the unfixed work, for obvious reasons.

When the minimum necessary fixing is completed the work should still be protected by a thick surrounding mount and glass or perspex covering,

touches the surface will to some degree disturb it and thus diminish the quality, the most effective protection is to place the work, untouched, into a mount, cover it with glass and frame it, taking care to seal the edges. The danger with this procedure is that even the slightest touch or jar will cause some pigment to fall off. Furthermore, and perhaps more importantly, the painter rarely retains the work and others will not know that it is still in its original delicate state, and might cause damage to it.

The only practical solution, therefore, is to apply some form of fixative to the surface. This is fraught with both difficulties and dangers although modern aerosols, lethal as some are to the environment, when used carefully do little damage and are quite effective.

The problem is that any rearrangement of the pigment on the surface, any diminution of the

29

Left: Rosalba Giovanna Carriera (1675–1757). *Portrait of a Man*
*c.*1720   Pastel on paper
57.8 × 47 cm (22³/₄ × 18¹/₂ in)
National Gallery, London
Carriera was born, worked and died in Venice. She was a portrait pastellist who painted many visitors on the Grand Tour through whom her reputation was spread in Europe. Her work is of the highest quality, precise and vivid in colour.

Opposite top: Maurice Quentin de la Tour (1704–1788). *Henry Dawkins*
*c.*1750   Pastel on paper
66.7 × 53.3 cm (26¹/₄ × 21 in)
National Gallery, London
La Tour was, with Carriera, the finest of the early pastellists whose work was widely popular. The quality and distinction of his drawing is apparent in this penetrating portrait.

Right: Odilon Redon. *Ophelia Among the Flowers*
1905–08   Pastel
64 × 91 cm (25¹/₂ × 35⁷/₈ in)
National Gallery, London

making sure that the pastel surface cannot come into contact with the glass. (Degas, it has to be said, was not always punctilious in this matter.) Artists' materials' manufacturers produce a range of fixatives which are adequate if used carefully.

Pastels repay great care. They are almost impossible to restore effectively but, if carefully maintained, they retain their brilliance and freshness almost indefinitely – as long as fugitive colours have not been used in their production (as for instance some coal tar dyes). Unfortunately, using manufacturers' ready-mades, you only discover any deficiencies some time afterwards.

In most art galleries the pastels from the 18th century or even earlier stand out from the walls in their brilliance as opposed to the darkening

surfaces of most oil paintings or the fading of watercolours.

Modern pastels can be said to date from the 18th century when pastel sticks were first generally manufactured by the artists themselves. Nevertheless, during the Renaissance some tinting of drawings with gum-bound colour occurred. Holbein's tinted drawings of Court figures during the reign of Henry VIII in England are very sensitive examples of the use of pastel effects. Pastel is, incidentally, very effective in the rendering of flesh and skin surfaces. A forerunner of pastel was the red chalk used by Leonardo da Vinci in many of his study drawings.

However, the method of pastel painting as it is known today, and was practised by Degas, was introduced and made popular in the early 18th century (1720s) notably by the Venetian painter Rosalba Carriera. The refined and delicate nature of pastel was especially attractive to Rococo taste and in her successors, Maurice Quentin de la Tour, Jean-Baptiste Perroneau and Jean Marc Nattier in France, and Anton Raphael Mengs in Germany, pastel reached its highest distinction before Degas.

In the 19th century Degas gave it a new vitality and diversity, making it almost uniquely his own special method. Other artists — both his contemporaries and earlier — had continued to use pastel, including both Delacroix and Jacques Louis David, but mostly as a means of quick investigatory studies. But for Degas it was a means of major exhibition works; as a result he is the most appropriate exemplar of the method for study.

Before Degas, pastel had employed the range of colours used in Renaissance *tempera* paintings such as those of Botticelli; some of La Tour's, for instance, have a light, colourful brilliance reminiscent of Baldovinetti's portraits. The colour range was from full hue to white with deep shades in the darks. Degas changed pastel painting into a contrasting colour brilliance which related to some of the Impressionist practices of, say, Pissarro or the later work of Gauguin.

31

Degas and Impressionism

It is the popular understanding that Degas was an Impressionist and it is important for any examination of his art to determine to what extent, if at all, this is true. There are a number of reasons why it is important to consider this, not the least being that 'Impressionism' as a word has such a strong hold on popular imagination that Degas' participation, or not, has some effect on the character of the movement.

There is always a natural tendency to convince oneself of what one believes should be the case; in this instance to discover qualities and characteristics in Degas' work which accord with our own understanding of Impressionism. It will almost certainly be Degas' own work which will have to some degree determined what that understanding will be. How far thus will the inclusion of Degas as an Impressionist be something of a self-fulfilling prophesy?

The name 'Impressionist' was coined by a critic who took it from a painting by, appropriately enough, Monet: *Impression — Sunrise*, which appeared at the first Impressionist exhibition. Degas himself always resisted the term 'Impressionist' being applied to him or his work and eventually succeeded in having the word 'Independent' replace 'Impressionist'. Nevertheless he was a prominent exhibitor in all but two of the group's shows. Since he sent a number of works (twenty-five to one show) each time, his work certainly contributed in no uncertain way to the impression that the shows were having. It should also be remembered that there were a number of exhibitors who were not Impressionists and it is thus reasonable to suppose that if he is included in the general understanding of the movement he must have seemed more akin and in sympathy than many of the other exhibitors. It seems unreasonable in these circumstances not to consider him as an Impressionist.

Nevertheless, when one examines his work in relation to that of those painters who are undeniably Impressionist, especially Monet, Pissarro

and Renoir, much of his work is of a different order and intention. Much of his painting practice, his attitude of mind and his pictorial philosophy is very different from theirs. In addition his subject matter is chosen for essentially different purposes. Thus, although his ballet dancers, for instance, are popularly supposed to be typically Impressionist, they are not.

To understand this some consideration of the beginnings of Impressionism may be helpful. The official art of the middle years of the 19th century in France held a dominant and autocratic position. Since the time of Louis XIV's Minister, Colbert, the French crown had always had a strong official hand on French culture and particularly the visual arts. From LeBrun to David under the Directoire

and later under Napoleon painters had held positions of almost dictatorial aesthetic authority in the art academic establishment. The rules and methods of study were set down with rigid finality and it was not possible to step outside them without seriously endangering one's artistic future or commercial success. French society and government, recognizing the propagandist value of this near monopoly, honoured and supported the conformist painters and sculptors. By the middle of the 19th century there was a unified social structure which supported conformists and virtually condemned nonconformists to failure. It was an evidently unsatisfactory situation, stultifying to creative imaginations and frustrating to young eager spirits. Some figures

Thomas Couture. *The Romans in the Time of Decadence* 1847   Oil on canvas 466 × 775 cm (183$\frac{1}{2}$ × 305$\frac{1}{8}$ in) Musée d'Orsay, Paris *Couture's painting is an accomplished example of the academic work of the time by a very successful exponent. Constructed on a simple picture-box-contained composition, the figures are effectively handled, many poses being taken from the work of other painters.*

such as Chardin and later Delacroix and Géricault showed determined and ultimately successful resistance supported in the early 1800s by the growth of Romanticism – particularly through the English poets and writers. The 1848 revolution, perhaps awakening memories of the destruction of the existing order fifty years earlier, acted as a catalyst in changing attitudes to an overweening academic authority. Thus, during the 1850s, groups such as the Barbizon painters in the forest around Fontainebleau, or individuals such as Courbet, opened possibilities which in the 1860s began to encourage a considerable number of 'independents' – that is, a number of painters who were prepared to stake their futures on working outside the academic teaching process. Their need was born and nurtured in the teaching ateliers of the great painters of the day.

The legacy of propagandist state art was an emphasis on subject matter and its clearly perceived message. The artistic justification lay in the subject and the elevating emotional or intellectual call to action it carried. Every picture told a story – usually moral. The story justified the painting and, although deficiency in the academic qualities of drawing, colour, composition, etc. ultimately spelled failure, the subject and clever way in which it was handled justified the work. The construction of the painting was essentially tonal. It should not be supposed that such works were either incompetent or ineffective. They had considerable impact on their society and their draughtsmanship was acquired by diligent study. The artists were educated, sensitive and cultured but they were programmed within the system.

Courbet, like his writer contemporaries Zola, Balzac and Flaubert, could not accept the academic restraints. His real interests lay elsewhere. Through his own individual strength of character and creative capacity he effected the beginning of a great release; the Impressionists eventually confirmed this in what, in hindsight, can be seen as the greatest revolution in painting since the Renaissance had redirected the course of European

Eugène Delacroix. *The Death of Sardanapulus*
1827 Oil on canvas
395 × 495 cm (155^1/$_2$ × 194^7/$_8$ in)
Musée du Louvre, Paris
Delacroix's painting, based on the poetic drama by Byron, the hero-figure of the Romantic movement, depicts the death of Sardanapulus surrounded by his concubines and horses who are being slaughtered before his eyes in advance of the destruction of his palace by fire. The whole restless action of the painting and its unusual compositional structure mark it as one of the great works of the French Romantic movement.

art. So effective was Impressionism that earlier paintings frequently assume an air of contemporary irrelevance, carrying only literary or historical interest. Additionally, they so far freed pictorial ambition that later painters have explored previously undreamed of areas of expression.

Always a difficult, awkward, forceful character, Courbet rejected both his early classical academic art training as well as the only acceptable alternative, the Romanticism of Delacroix. His strong socialist philosophy, his deeply ingrained feeling for nature drawn from his early life in Ornans in the Franche Compte, his distaste for social pretensions and the inflated art that it seemed to him it spawned, led him to an apparently uncompromising realism. His early paintings reflect the rural life in Ornans and its inhabitants in such works as *The Burial at Ornans* (*Funèbre à Ornans*, 1849), quite out of feeling with contemporary taste. His paint handling was direct and unsensuous. His later paintings caused great scandal, particularly a number of nudes of a seemingly unromanticized realism. His political opinions and the actions they prompted got him into serious trouble with the authorities and his last years were spent in unhappy exile while his property in France was confiscated to pay some debts claimed by the state — a sorry and unedifying story.

Courbet's importance for Impressionism lay in two main factors. Firstly his approach to his subject matter was direct, concerned with contemporary everyday events and carried an underlying care for the accessibility of the work to the public; the

Gustave Courbet. *The Burial at Ornans*
1849   Oil on canvas
314 × 665 cm (123⅝ × 261⅞ in)
Musée d'Orsay, Paris
In marked contrast to both Couture and Delacroix, Courbet has taken a common experience to present, with apparent sombre realism, the familiar grief accompanying death. The large frieze-like painting reveals his deep social concern.

viewer needed no literary or historical knowledge to get the message. This, incidentally, did not endear his work to those who had such knowledge and expected to use it in discussion of works of art with their peers. The effect of all this was to diminish the importance of the subject. The second factor of importance to Impressionism is found in Courbet's paint handling. Although still essentially a tonal painter, trained in academic methods and having a great admiration for the masters from Michelangelo to Rembrandt, his manipulation of paint gave an emphasis to the surface of the painting. This began the process, carried further by the Impressionists, of a painting being seen for itself, as a direct placing of the understanding and form of the subject on the surface with paint. While this may seem at first

sight the obvious intention of any painter it was not so in the art atmosphere of the mid-19th century. It struck a blow for creative independence that was attractive to the young restless painters of the day — those who were to become the 'Independents' of the 1860s, Degas among them. Courbet was thus a proto-protagonist of the modern pictorial revolution.

This was properly initiated by the Impressionists. When one recalls what pictorial investigations, experiments and adventures have taken place in this century the truly revolutionary nature of Impressionism becomes apparent. Equally apparent is that Degas is not central to this. It is, incidentally, a curious feature of current criticism that the movement which sponsored the modern investigatory freedom should have become the

Claude Monet. *Melting Ice on the River Seine*
1881   Oil on canvas
59 × 98.5 cm (23 $\frac{1}{5}$ × 38 $\frac{3}{4}$ in)
Sammlung Oskar Reinhart Am Römmerholz, Winterthur
One of a series of canvases of this subject made from sketches Monet made on the spot in a few hours in January 1880. Monet is popularly and accurately regarded as the archetypal Impressionist.

exemplar of the acceptable by those who criticize it.

A number of other influences were important to those who were to become the Impressionists. There were the fresh, lively paintings of Boudin and Jongkind, the Barbizon painters with their direct approach to landscape and, perhaps most influential, the paintings of Turner which Monet and Pissarro saw during their visit to England at the time of the Franco–Prussian war. There was

also the Japanese colour print which, in 1867, at the Paris World's Fair, the painters encountered for the first time. Bracquemond, an engraver friend of Degas', was the first to introduce the colour print and *japonisme* became the rage, inspiring a number of painters notably Whistler and Tissot, both known to Degas, to a sort of *japonaiserie*. The Impressionists were influenced by the whole idea of Japanese design and its two-dimensionality.

The combination of these influences on the young Impressionists, together with their own creative temperaments, was responsible for a quietly inflexible determination to find an art which reflected all this. Degas, it must be admitted, should be excepted from this. They had a number of friends of independently similar mind whose solutions were different but were viewed sympathetically by the Impressionists. They were never an exclusive club or defined group; they owed no allegiance, avowed or implicit, to each other or to any idea or philosophy called 'Impressionism'. They pursued individually — and mostly separately — their own artistic vision, more or less influenced by the factors noted above. Thus while Impressionism is real it is as difficult to pin down as ideas usually are. What may be claimed is that Manet, Monet, Pissarro, Sisley, Renoir and Degas all contributed to a greater or lesser extent to the Impressionist revolution. Their friends and fellow painters, some of whom later adopted Impressionist methods, did not participate even though they

Left: *Louis Jacques Daguerre* (1789–1851)
1845   Photograph
This early photograph by one of the founders of photography reveals him with clarity in a typical painterly pose. It is not surprising that many painters were disconcerted by the invention — although they did not include Degas who became an enthusiastic amateur photographer.

Opposite top: *American Civil War: General Grant and his Staff*
1861–65   Photograph
Within 20 years of its discovery photography was widely used to record events, and among the most vivid images at the time were those of the American Civil War.

42

exhibited with them in the Impressionist exhibitions. Monet is popularly and accurately regarded as the archetypal Impressionist but even he does not represent every aspect of its nature.

The only painter listed above but who did not exhibit in the Impressionist exhibitions was Manet and he does stand somewhat apart in a role between Courbet who influenced him and Degas who never considered himself an Impressionist. Manet's importance to Impressionism was that he provided a focus for the dissatisfied young painters. He had become a centre of revolt, without any such wish on his part, since 1863 when his painting *Déjeuner sur l'Herbe* was the subject of a critical storm at the Salon des Refusés. His pictorial method of *peinture claire* became an anti-academic alternative and had some effect on later Impressionist technique. It should not be supposed, however, as is often assumed, that *peinture claire* is part of the Impressionist method.

Recognizing that a definition is not accurately attainable we may now nevertheless attempt some description of the character and importance of the movement. Impressionism was a convention of pictorial expression based upon an interpretation of visual perception in terms of colour. Although there are a number of important but less critical aspects of Impressionist painting, it was the use of colour which was at the basis of the revolution. Their perception that paintings could be constructed in hue rather than tone and that vision provided information that was not traditionally used was the basis for a new painting palette. This is the single most important element. Accompanying this, and arising from their temperamental antagonism towards the established academic approach, they abandoned the literary for the everyday and the contemporary as subject matter. They also perceived that natural form as revealed by light was usually in a state of visual change so that constructing in tone and line was inadequate. When landscape was considered it was discovered that further movement, of trees, foliage, water, etc., presented the everyday scene in an everchanging state. The overall result was to raise the colour key, reduce the definition of form, and translate tone into colour.

Degas' relationship with these characteristics is, in fact, somewhat tenuous. His pictorial construction remained tonally based. He was not concerned with visual effects of light and colour and his palette was never 'Impressionist'. His drawing was linearly, indeed classically, based. His approach to composition was careful, intellec-

tual and inventive. He made many preliminary sketches for all his major paintings. These characteristics are essentially different from most Impressionist practices and since they cover the main aspects of any painting it is evident that Degas had different intentions from the other Impressionists.

At the same time he was concerned with everyday subject matter and his work is often designed to create an 'impression' rather than to present a 'finished' work. The processes of his creation are left still revealed which has the effect of implying an immediacy which may be far from the truth. Like other members of the group he is concerned with the availability of his subject. Despite his classical and academic background his chosen subjects were very much part of the direct experiences of his life. Perhaps, as with his horse and jockey paintings, his subjects were not those of his friends, but they were equally not those of his academic contemporaries.

It is perhaps best to leave the question open. As has been noted he is always associated with the Impressionist group and is likely to continue to be so, but it is perhaps worth noting that the earliest historian of the Impressionist development, Théodore Duret, does not include Degas as a major Impressionist.

There is an important technological development to consider here since Degas' response to it was different from most of the Impressionists. In the year of Degas' birth, 1834, Fox Talbot in England began his experiments which succeeded in producing fixed photographic negatives on paper. In France somewhat earlier work had been done by Niepce (who died in 1833) and Daguerre so that by 1839 both Daguerre and Fox Talbot had independently developed methods of fixing a photographic image derived directly from the tonal pattern supplied by the subject. The sensitivity of the process enabled the photographer from the beginning to achieve a tonal pattern which reflected the subject with great if limited accuracy – and with no 'artistic' abilities. From the American Civil War the photograph became an essential part of the recording of events with an immediacy and accuracy previously unknown.

The Impressionists thus grew up with photography as later generations have grown up with radio, cinema and television – as an accepted,

unquestioned part of common experience. They did not see it either as a threat or as a special opportunity. Some were attracted to it as an aid to their work; others were little interested.

For the academics, trained in tonal pictorial construction, its appearance seemed an unmitigated disaster. Paul Delaroche, an early 19th century academic, observed despairingly on first seeing a photographic image that 'from today painting is dead'. Some solace was initially drawn from the belief that colour remained unattainable in photography but this was short lived as in 1861 the first true colour photograph was obtained by the famous physicist, James Clerk Maxwell. Thus before the Impressionist revolution the creation of both tonal and colour patterns by photographic means was possible, although it was not until the 1890s that colour photography became a practical proposition.

However, by the 1860s tonal photography was such an accepted feature of image making that it had an influence – sometimes directly, sometimes obliquely – on the course of the Impressionist movement. It did, for instance, emphasize the colour nature of vision and, as the speed of making

photographs increased, it offered unusual compositional suggestions.

Degas' own response to photography was enthusiastic. He, more than others of the 'Independents', used the camera for information, for compositional ideas and as a means of storing impressions. In his later years, as his eyesight deteriorated, he relied increasingly on photography as a means of close examination of potential subject matter. His drawing ability was of such quality and assurance that he did not fear, but could effectively use, the camera. His pictorial sense of space and action accorded well with the 'snapshot' element in photography. When, later, Marey and Muybridge demonstrated through photography the true action of the horse in motion

Eadweard Muybridge. *Horses in Motion*
1887   Photograph
This sequence of the horse's galloping action reveals for the first time that the traditional depiction was inaccurate.

Claude Monet. *Grain Stacks. End of Summer*
1891   Oil on canvas
60 × 100 cm (23⅝ × 39⅜ in)
Musée d'Orsay, Paris
Monet's use of vivid colours in shaded areas
of his high-key paintings can be seen in this
example.

he was fascinated and responded immediately in his work. His are the first paintings which show the accurate stages in a horse's moving limbs.

The effect on other painters, including the Impressionists, was also, in the long run, profound. It emphasized the point that direct representation was not of itself necessarily art — certainly not 'high' art — and was, or might be, mere facility. The presentation of tonal images at least was mechanical and technological. How could it be possible, they wondered, that 'artistic' statements could be made mechanically? Could an image of the kind that 'told a story' be effectively undertaken by the camera? The photographers certainly tried to establish that it could and that they too were 'artists'. Some of their quaint attempts at classical compositions using nudes to represent gods and goddesses have now acquired a period charm but they served only to diminish the authority of contemporary academic painters. Degas himself was very conscious of what the camera could and could not contribute to his painting.

While Degas, therefore, remains on the periphery of the Impressionist movement he was nevertheless uniquely able to promote some aspects of Impressionist philosophy. His social background and academic training, his historical early work, and the distinction, early recognized, of his drawing, secured him an acceptance in art circles which, in the early years, only Manet equalled. His vicious conversational wit was fascinating and his identification with the Impressionists gave them some additional credence among the independents and writers of the café society at, for instance, the Nouvelle Athènes. And his subject matter was in sympathy with the other Impressionists. After his early historical academic essays his subjects were chosen from contemporary life. His nudes, particularly, placed him outside the acceptable tradition and linked him more with the 'Independents'. Portrayed in unguarded and, as they supposed, unobserved moments, engaged in private rituals of bathing and such associated activities, they seem too real and earthy for 'high' academic art.

Again his concern with movement, the incidental, the fleeting moment, the passing show and the unusual optical effects with which they provide him, link him again with the interests of the other members of the group. To this extent his work contributes to the overall popular pattern

image of Impressionism without which the understanding of it would be diminished. To this extent he is part of Impressionism.

Something more should be said of his use of colour and his palette. Degas' colour was not typically Impressionist. Nor was the tonal pictorial construction of most of his work. He constructed his paintings and pastels as tonal images using local colour only. He does not find, at least visually, blues, mauves or purples in the shadows; for him the less illuminated areas are tonally dark, not 'colourful', as for instance is found in the shaded side of a Monet *Grain Stack* painting. Thus in his work the passages of tonal difference do not carry a message of varying hues and the compositional

structure is consequently tonal and, since his use of line must also be included, linear. Since, furthermore, a tonally constructed image tends to break up the picture plane into expressions of depth his work does not lay emphasis on the surface of the painting as does the painting of, say, Monet or Pissarro. It is perhaps, as has been noted, this element that most distinguishes him ultimately from the true Impressionist group. This distinction is most evident in his portraits which come closer to the academic paintings of Ingres, whom he much admired, than to, say, Renoir.

When Degas is considered in isolation, away from the movement, his individualism and true stature can be evaluated. He was one of the great draughts-men of Western art, to be considered alongside such figures as Raphael, Michelangelo, Watteau and Ingres. He was a uniquely inventive composer of pictures. He had the ability, common only to the greatest, of making a subject and his vision of it especially his and acceptably part of the history of painting as did Goya, Rembrandt and Turner.

For Degas art was a cultural, intellectual activity proper to the higher levels of human achievement, to be carried on privately in a studio; it was not a commonplace, popularly focused entertainment for the masses. He did not have a desire to please but only a wish to discover and express the deepest understanding of which he was capable. In the last analysis he was, thus, not an Impressionist.

Analysis and Consideration of Main Subjects

The Bellelli Family
(*La famille Bellelli*)
(pastel study)
c.1858   Pastel and pencil on paper
55 × 63cm (21⅝ × 24¾in)
Ordrupgaard Museum
Copenhagen

In the detail below, Degas shows the advantages of drawing in pastel. The broad areas of single tonal value show the simplicity of the medium, at its best when blocking in broad areas of colour.

Degas visited the Bellelli family in Florence in August 1858 and while there made studies for the group portrait which he completed in Paris on his return in April 1859.

A number of his family lived in Italy (Naples and Florence) and he liked to visit them for extended periods. He was particularly fond of his Aunt Laura who was married to Gennaro Bellelli, a successful lawyer living in Florence, with two daughters. Bellelli was a supporter of Cavour and an enthusiast for the unification of Italy. In 1861 he became a Senator for the Kingdom of Italy and Director of the Postal and Telegraphic system but he died soon after his appointment. At the time of Degas' visit the family was

The Bellelli Family
(La famille Bellelli)
c.1858–60   Oil on canvas
200 × 250cm (78¾ × 98½in)
Musée d'Orsay
Paris

in mourning for the death of a son and in the same year, 1858, the Baroness had lost her father, Degas' grandfather.

Degas was very much at home with this family and said that he was much too well treated to work as he would have liked. He was greatly taken with his young cousins and the portrayal of the group seems undoubtedly to have been a labour of love. It was also originally intended only to include his aunt and the two children. As the composition progressed, carefully constructed with many preparatory sketches of the whole group, single poses

and details, Degas decided to include his uncle in the painting. He had some misgivings about this since, as seems likely from his portrait, Gennaro's temper was unpredictable.

In Paris he combined all the sketches he had made into the finished composition which became his first major group painting. It is early evidence of the care with which Degas always constructed his paintings. It has all the presence of an Ingres in its attention to the placing of details and in the precision of the drawing in the figures. It is interesting to note how

much more sympathetic the portrait of Laura is in the pastel than in the finished oil painting. Her expression in the painting is mask-like, forbidding and withdrawn, while in the pastel it is gentle and friendly. It is difficult to explain this difference since there was no change as far as is known in Degas' own feelings towards his aunt.

While considering the differences between the pastel and the oil painting it will be noted that the dog is not included in the pastel study, there are no studies for it and seems an afterthought — unlikely as this is.

The composition of the worked out pastel study, as well as the oil painting, has some revelatory elements contained in it. In both, Laura is linked with her children but separated from her husband, whose gaze crosses the picture but does not link with hers. In both pastel and oil she seems to look beyond him into the distance. It is known that their arranged marriage was not an easy one and some suggestion of antagonism may be intended by Degas.

Laura, in her forties, was pregnant while this pastel was painted and this is implied in

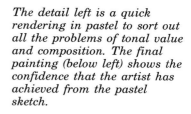

The detail left is a quick rendering in pastel to sort out all the problems of tonal value and composition. The final painting (below left) shows the confidence that the artist has achieved from the pastel sketch.

both the form of the dress and the quiet maturity of her gentle musing look. Had Degas, one wonders, heard something to cause him to change the look by the time he came to undertake the oil painting later in Paris? Laura's younger daughter, while looking towards her father, is not looking at him and, like her mother's, her gaze seems focused in space. Degas thought the elder daughter beautiful and portrays her looking forward towards him. The pastel shows her, too, much more gentle than does the oil.

Compositionally, both the pastel and the oil are based on a series of interlocked rectangles against which the figures offer a curving linear pattern. The two aprons provide startling light key

Above: *The Bellelli Family* Study. Pen and wash
Degas made many studies for all his portraits; some finished, some slight sketches, and some in pastel to determine the composition. This pen-and-wash drawing of the younger Bellelli daughter is a lively example.

notes in the essentially low key painting. The preparatory pastel has been used to work out the tonal pattern of the subsequent oil.

Degas' pastel technique was already assured and controlled. His drawing of the heads, for instance, is careful and precise over the pencil underdrawing. Although not finished it is clear that the total intention is already in Degas' mind.

The following two landscape
pastels are from a small
number that Degas made after
a visit with Manet to
Boulogne and St. Valery-en-
Caux, Villers-sur-Mer, Etretat
and the beach at Beuzeval.

Generally Degas expressed
no great regard for landscapes
and landscape painting but he
was in fact more interested
than he admitted. He executed
a number of pastels – and a
few watercolours – as a result
of his visits into the country-
side in France and Italy. As
might be expected he was not
one to sit down in the open
air and paint and draw 'on
site' as it were. Most, if not
all, of his landscapes are
painted in the studio,
recollected in tranquillity. His
interest was, as ever,
intellectual.

Although made in his
studio, these works, nevertheless, have a direct freshness.
They seem on the spot
notations in their affinity with
those of Boudin and to some
extent have the natural
authority found in the studies
of Courbet. The quality shown
in these early works in pastel,
simply and directly drawn as
they are, deserves attention
although they neither figure
largely in his work nor are
characteristically understood
to be a feature of his subject
matter.

They are straightforward
pastels drawn on toned paper
and showing more surface
manipulation to achieve an
atmospheric effect than is
common in Degas' use of
pastel for other subjects. They
are not detailed and show him
realizing images from a highly
retentive mental store. In this
respect they are certainly
'impressions' and, like
common Impressionist works,
they are full of an effect of
atmosphere. To some extent
they remind one of some
paintings of Monet.

Houses by the Seaside
(Maisons au bord de la mer)
1869 Pastel on paper
31.4 × 46.5cm (12⅜ × 18¼in)
Cabinet des Dessins
Musée du Louvre
Paris

Cliffs by the Sea
(Falaises au bord de la mer)
1869   Pastel on paper
32.4 × 46.9cm (12¾ × 18½in)
Cabinet des Dessins
Musée du Louvre
Paris

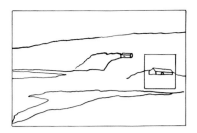

Detail of Houses by the Seaside. *This pastel painting, very much Impressionistic in style, shows the simplicity of laying down clean colours in basic planes, with only the tonal values suggesting detail and perspective.*

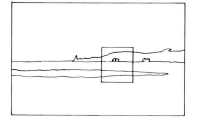

Detail of Cliffs by the Sea. *As with the detail opposite, this painting shows the same qualities taken a stage further where the pastel rendering is dominant.*

*Edmond Duranty
(Duranty)*
1879   Gouache and pastel on
canvas
100 × 100cm (39⅜ × 39⅜in)
Burrell Collection
Glasgow
Scotland

*In this painting, Degas
demonstrates his ability to
explore in mixed media —
gouache and pastel. The
details opposite show the
contrasting styles of the Van
Gogh-like rendering of the
faces and the broad gouache
techniques of the background.*

Duranty was one of the number of writers and artists who had frequented the Café Guerbois and who had transferred their allegiance to the Nouvelle Athènes in the Place Pigalle. By the time this pastel was completed he had known Degas and the other habitués of both cafés for a number of years. Louis Emile Edmond Duranty was a critic and novelist, publicly unsuccessful but critically respected, who earned his living as a journalist and was an art critic for the *Gazette des Beaux Arts*. Although a follower of Courbet's friend Champfleury he was less concerned with the socialist principles of either of them than with their devotion to realism and their observations about contemporary life. Degas was greatly influenced by Duranty and they became good friends. After Duranty's death in 1880, Degas arranged the formalities and made strenuous efforts to assist his widow by a sale of works donated by his friends. Degas is mentioned by name in Duranty's novel *Le peintre Louis Martin*.

Duranty's writings on art included a brochure called *La Nouvelle Peinture*, which was an effective defence of the Impressionists so that to some extent he may be regarded as the theorist of the movement.

In this brilliant, large-scale, pastel and gouache painting Degas has displayed a mastery of mixed technique. Watercolour has been used as an underpainting, partly obscured by overpainting in gouache (distemper) and pastel – particularly evident in the head and hands but occurring in small touches elsewhere in the work. The books on the shelves are mainly painted in opaque colour over watercolour, while powdered pastel mixed with water has been used for the books and manuscripts piled on the table.

The surroundings of books and papers, which may have suggested to Cézanne his own use of a similar setting for his portrait of Geffroy, were Duranty's own books and they provide an original setting for the sensitive, pensive face of the writer from which emanates some intimation of the insecurity of his life. As is usual with Degas there are a number of studies leading to the final work. His brilliance

in suggesting character and feeling is very evident in this work as is Degas' own sympathy and affection for the writer.

Nevertheless, perhaps the greatest interest is in the ensemble itself. The composition, placing the sitter below eyelevel (at about the shelf immediately above his head) and thus introducing a steep forward perspective, is carefully conceived to suggest involvement of an intimate observer who must be standing close to the front of the desk. The ordered rows of books behind the sitter – suggesting perhaps the ordered world of completed work – contrast with the bulky, irregular, disorganized clutter of work in progress. In the middle, sharply defined, is the subject. But while the close drawing of the figure lays emphasis upon itself, the whole corner of the room and its contents are equally significant in the composition. The confined, almost claustrophobic, pressing in on the writer of these elements suggests his creative isolation and intellectual remoteness.

One feels Degas' interest in his subject emotionally and as part of a greater pictorial plan.

The Chorus (*Choriste*)
1877   Pastel on monotype
29 × 30cm (11⅜ × 11¾in)
Musée d'Orsay
Paris

This small, freely handled pastel over a monotype is a good example of a frequent practice of Degas'. A painting on glass which had reached a fair degree of resolution was transferred to paper with an inevitably reduced definition but retaining the full character of the original composition. The colour would have been somewhat muted in the process and the tonal range reduced so that a new unity of softness would have been obtained. To this was added a pastel overlay which, because the composition was established, could be treated freely. Strong and vibrant colours laid on boldly are included. Degas is here exploring the effect of the foot-lights in changing the emphasis of the forms, of simplifying effects and providing a dramatic sense of the lighting.

The work was one of twenty-four that Degas showed at the third Impressionist exhibition which clearly indicates that the free pastel strokes and loosely applied colour should not mislead anyone into believing that this was a rough sketch for some later finished work. Indeed, although there are other such footlight subjects, none is close enough to be directly related.

It is perhaps appropriate to recall again here that the use of a monotype base reverses the original image and provides the painter with a new composition upon which to work. Since a number of the pastels considered here are on a monotype base, Degas must have found the opportunities provided attractive. Further consideration of the method will be found when other subjects are discussed.

Degas' interest in the ballet, which remained with him for the rest of his working life, began on his return from his visit to New Orleans in 1873. From this time, until his sight became so bad that he could no longer work directly from the subject, he made frequent visits to the Opera. His last works on the ballet, all pastels, date from about 1903.

So commanding and original are his theatre and ballet works that any mention of art and ballet immediately recalls Degas to mind. Although many artists have been attracted by the ballet no

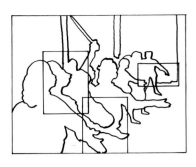

In the details of this painting, the pure genius of Degas can be clearly seen. Rendered on top of a monotype, his bold use of colour avoids the need for mannerisms.

other painter or sculptor has become, like Degas, synonymous with the subject. And yet such exclusive identification is both misleading and diminishing since in many respects Degas' interest lay very little in ballet itself. Indeed it would be true to say that he rarely portrays any specific ballet; one would, indeed, scarcely expect him to do so since the emphasis on a precise narrative message would have been at variance with his desire to establish significant generalizations of a recollected reality. Incidentally it might be worth noting that oxymorons characterize many of the attempts to identify the nature of Degas' art – such as 'realistic fictions' (Huyghe), 'lyrical cruelty' (Fauré) and 'visionary analysis' (Focillon).

It is also unfairly limiting – for a deeper reason – to consider Degas only as a ballet painter. While ballet was an important source of his intellectual pictorial research material, it was only one of a number of sources all of which had considerable importance to him in his search for a tradition-based modernity.

Other subjects and other ballet pastels to be considered later will explore this further.

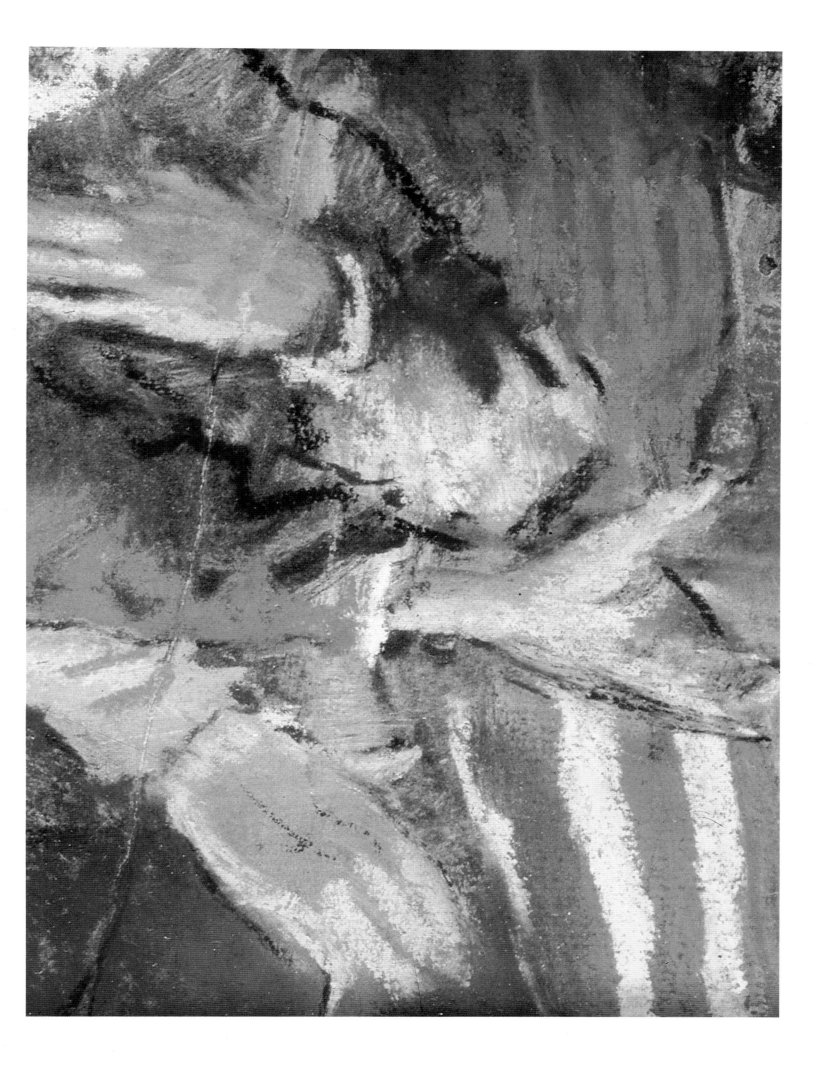

In the early 1860s Degas made his first studies of horses in motion, while he was still concerned with history painting. He was praised by Puvis de Chavannes in 1865 for his scene of war in the Middle Ages which contained, as did most of his history paintings, careful posed studies of horses.

Partly as a result of very modest success in his submissions to the Salon and partly as a reflection of his dissatisfaction with such historical subject matter, Degas was already searching about for some more relevant and contemporary source of new inspiration. In the horse he found an ideal subject; one which, before and since Degas, has inspired artists of a great variety of visual interests. A traditional subject with classical associations, the horse still continued to be an important feature of 19th century social and commercial life. In different circumstances it could become a symbol of strength and energy, or of the depressed and oppressed, or even of the victim as, for instance, in Picasso's *Guernica.* In 19th century France it continued to be the subject of sculptures and paintings and was, significantly, acceptable to Salon juries. The great Romantics of the early years of the century, Géricault and Delacroix, painted horses with a fiery energy, symbolizing passion with an almost anthropomorphic intensity.

Degas needed a modern contemporaneous twist to the subject and found it in the elegant delicacy of the highly bred racehorse — a reflection perhaps of his own perception of himself rather than as a commonplace commercial

Jockeys in the Rain
(*Jockeys sous la pluie*)
Late 1880s Pastel on paper
47 × 65cm (18½ × 25⅝in)
Burrell Collection
Glasgow
Scotland

Overleaf. *Here Degas shows the economies of using pastel. The unusual composition, which is little more than a rough sketch, is brought together only by the tonal highlights.*

workhorse. The society horse, engaged, like a workhorse, in the service of man – but social man – may have had a conscious appeal to Degas. He would have been aware that only for him, and Manet among his artist friends, would the racecourse have been a comfortable subject. Nevertheless, like the ballet, it was a daily activity but of a special distinguishing kind, full of colour and action. It was also the sport of that section of society that might be expected to buy paintings and be attracted by the subject. All in all, a clever choice and, as it turned out, a successful one, for his racehorse paintings became very popular.

In 1866 he exhibited *The*

Wounded Jockey at the Salon – his first and not entirely successful essay on the subject. The horse, one notes, is painted in the 18th century traditional sporting print pose with all its legs inaccurately spreadeagled. It was only later, as already noted, from the photographs of Marey and Muybridge that Degas, like everyone else, learned of the correct motion of the running horse.

The racecourse of Longchamp, then in the Bois de Boulogne and in easy reach of the centre of Paris, had been founded in 1856 and was the best in France. By the 1860s it had already become part of the social round and Degas began to attend the races, to observe, sketch and construct compositions.

In *Jockeys in the Rain* and *Jockeys Before the Race*, Degas also seems to show some influence of Japanese prints where the simplicity and precision of the composition and definition of form call up echoes of the print making process. *Jockeys in the Rain* has a brilliant and daring compositional construction,

almost all the action being confined to the top right sector defined by the diagonal. The dense cross-hatching of the pastel in the lower section is carefully constructed to create a 'flat' conscious recession. The drawing of the horses is precisely patterned, being built up from sketches and drawings, some of them made much earlier (late 1860s to early 1870s). The watery effect of the rain is beautifully suggested and the whole work is a brilliant example of Degas' compositional inventiveness and superb draughtsmanship.

Jockeys Before the Race is another bold example of composition – much of the scene as it would have been perceived being left to the imagination in the interests of a dramatic and unusual image. The device of the foreground post as a division of the picture area, concentrating the action on the right and again leaving over half of the picture area 'unused', is characteristic of Degas' inventive compositional approach. The post, incidentally, has the same

effect as the high viewpoint in the Duranty pastel, of drawing the observer into a close and precise relationship to the action. It has a further effect, of which Degas was well aware, of suggesting the 'snapshot' effect – of the work not being composed at all, caught almost by accident, so that the 'photographer', in concentrating on the horses, has not noticed the post. This gives an unusual immediacy and sense of actuality to the scene although, as we know, it was very carefully constructed.

It will be noticed that this work is in essence on cardboard. The method is noted elsewhere (see page 23) but it is also worth noting at this point that it gives a clean freshness and directness to the work.

The jockey and horse on the extreme right in both works show a similarity of pose and treatment that suggests they are the result of the same original study. This indicates Degas' well known habit of working out a pose in the studio and of working from drawings.

Jockeys Before the Race
(*Avant la course*)
1879 Essence on cardboard
180 × 74cm (70⅞ × 29⅛in)
Barber Institute of Fine Arts
University of Birmingham
England

The endearment of this picture
is in its composition. Although
Degas has used an economy
of style (as shown in the
details) and the painting is less
refined than others of his, it is
nevertheless a masterpiece in
execution.

Racehorses in Training
(*Chevaux de course:*
l'entraînement)
1894 Pastel on paper
48 × 64cm (18⅞ × 25in)
Thyssen-Bornemisza Collection
Lugano
Switzerland

Degas
94

*The details overleaf show just
how brilliant an artist Degas
was. Although this picture is
small by modern-day
standards, any part of it could
be cut up and stand as a work
of art in its own right.
Obviously painted on a tonal
background, the colours
literally sing for attention.*

70

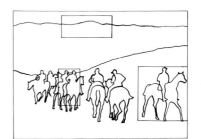

Degas' practice of constructing a work out of studies rather than from an actual scene is evident in this closely knit pastel. While there is a strong sense of actuality in this brilliant colourful work, the constructed relationships and grouping happen quite independently of the landscape so that the figures seem a sort of superimposed frieze. The distant mountains are drawn with a vibrant light touching their tops which has the effect of placing the rest of the scene in an indirect, tonally subdued, unifying pattern, although the actual fall of light, particularly in relation to the horses, is not expressed naturally or observed correctly. No attempt has indeed been made to examine the colour or tonal effect; the dark area, in its tonal relationship with the top of the distant hills and the far horses and jockeys, is carefully calculated to link them pictorially while continuing the 'flattening' effect of the foreground grass and mid-distance hillock. The space and effect of distance in the pastel is thus controlled, constructed and unnatural. At the same time it is singularly convincing — one can determine the distances between the horses and their relationship with the scenery (a theatrical backdrop?), whilst recognizing that, for instance, the hillock does not recess naturally.

Most particularly one also notes that the scene has not been conceived or presented in terms of aerial perspective. There is no sense of air or atmosphere and the effect of these on colour — an essential preoccupation of Monet and the other Impressionists. This is very apparent in the colours of the jockeys which, in actuality, would have appeared much muted and 'blued' in the distance represented.

All this is evidence on the one hand of Degas' studio construction, that the work

was not done *en plein air*, and, on the other, of Degas' remoteness from much Impressionist preoccupation with the effects of aerial perspective.

The composition and treatment are both un-Impressionist. The composition, a banded frieze with carefully grouped but seemingly casual horses and riders, is balanced, as are the colour and tonal oppositions. The treatment of the colour is somewhat more dense than in many of his pastels. The surface is highly worked; the dark dull green paper is almost covered by short sharp strokes or dots of colour, and, in certain parts, worked over again (e.g. behind the right hand horse or on the dark hill area) with a point or possibly a stump. Degas was an experimenter who worked as it occurred to him, so that many different ways of achieving his effects are found in his work. It is also difficult sometimes to determine, as in this case, exactly how the result is obtained.

The colour has an unusual intensity in the top half of the hills and Denys Sutton, in his admirable study of Degas, has suggested that echoes of Odilon Redon may be discerned. At all events this pastel is an example of Degas at his most intellectual. It should also be noted that this is a late work, produced when he was certainly suffering considerably from the difficulties of his declining sight.

73

The Green Room at the Opera
(*Le foyer de la danse*)
c.1882 Pastel on board
58 × 83cm (22¾ × 32⅔in)
Burrell Collection
Glasgow
Scotland

The details overleaf show Degas at his best. Working on a dark background from dark to light, this picture is brought to life purely by the light coming through the window.

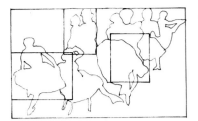

The Opera was a favourite haunt of Degas'. Apart from his frequent visits to performances, he spent time backstage (although perhaps not as much as his continued treatment of the subject suggests), in the wings and dressing rooms, making sketches and pose notations, usually of single figures. From these he constructed, in his studio, more elaborate compositions containing a number of figures. In these the ballet dancers, their dressers, their friends and families, the ballet masters and assistants all appear in much considered groupings, each engaged in their separate and different activities: one tying a shoe, another adjusting a shoulder strap, in receiving instructions or in conversation, or just waiting for their call. In other examples the dancers are on stage, taking a bow, in the middle of a dance step, or waiting in the wings to go on.

In most of these the painter depicts them in actions not seen by the public or not from the public viewpoint. He takes the observer behind the scene, gives him a private secret view. Sometimes this enhances the glamour of the scene, lends enchantment in a frozen moment which the viewers in the stalls cannot see or cannot hold in their conscious memory. At other times, behind the scenes, he shows the mundane actions which precede or follow the public performance, revealing the dancers as young, often gauche, girls, hardworking, not always attractive or intelligent and usually much younger and less sophisticated than they appear on stage.

These elaborated compositions were, like the horse and jockey paintings, all constructed in his studio. The lively originality of the figure disposition, the manipulation of space and distance, the controlled use of colour and tone combine to give these works a visual authority

although they rarely represent an actual scene.

Many of them are in pastel and are in varying degrees of finish; the latest of them show the effect of his failing vision. Those from the 1870s and early 1880s are the most fully worked.

The Green Room is not an example of high finish but it has a quality of sentiment together with a distinction of drawing that makes it one of his most interesting ballet pastels. The figure above is fully worked, beautifully compositionally balanced, one of his most elegantly perceived and drawn figures. She is in fact slightly off balance and needs the support of the chair back as she adjusts her shoe, isolated in her own private activity. The other figures are less finished but are each equally isolated in reflection or association with one other, possibly a mother or aunt as chaperone. The sense of reality and feeling, affection, nervousness, introspection are all strikingly conveyed.

The composition is also typically inventive; the steep angle, as has been noted earlier, conveys a sense of involvement of the observer in the action.

Dancers Preparing for an Audition
(*Examen de danse*)
c.1880 Pastel on paper
63.4 × 48.2cm (25 × 19in)
Denver Art Museum
Denver
Colorado

As in the previous painting, the figures in this composition are isolated — here each in the private world of anticipation and apprehension.

Degas has presented the subject as if it was suddenly revealed to him, which in his haste to capture it has led him to cut off the figures at the edges. Of course, this is in some ways the essence of the hasty snapshot and Degas' interest in photography has already been noted. However, in this connection there is a further point to make. In the early days of photography the exposure time was so long that a snapshot of a moving scene was not possible — a portrait photograph was indeed a testing experience requiring a long period of total immobility on the part of the sitter. By the 1880s, when this pastel was executed, the speed of the camera enabled relatively quick images to be captured and Degas used the effect quite consciously in a number of his compositions, including this one.

Although it looks like a snapshot it is of course as usual carefully considered as a composition for precisely the effect it gives. The faces carry the emotion of the scene, explaining the title, and Degas has arranged the figures for their dramatic effect, bunching three heads into the top right hand corner. If he had been really interested primarily in their emotional state before an audition he might have been expected to have brought them more into the centre stage of the painting. But the effect of the very tight grouping, almost in the margin, has some psychological identity with the withdrawn feeling of a separate but common intention, imbued with competition, that such an occasion must evoke. To pursue the matter a little further, the fact that the figures are on the right and cut off against a wall with a presumed movement left towards the stage implies a movement

against rather than with the tide — remembering the Western world's left to right visual habit. Imagine the composition reversed and the difference will be immediately apparent.

The classical ballet dress has a lightness and delicacy which the pastel method is very suited to capture. Its linear directional fall can quickly and effectively be expressed in a few pastel strokes while the close and subtle colour gradations very

expressively capture the form. The solidity of the colour, combined with variations of direction in linear drawing, is also visually seductive as can be seen, for instance, in the area around the blue sash bow.

The buff ground colour of the paper is visible in the lower half (floor area) while the wall is a more positive yellow. This looks a flat area of colour almost without linear texture and this is achieved by the use of either

fingers or a stump working over the surface after the colour has been drawn on. By the slight variation of colour sticks mixed by fingers or stump a very lively colour effect is achieved.

It should be noted that Degas draws each of the heads differently to suit his purpose. He clearly does not want the same emphasis on the left-hand edge and the head on this side is simply sketched although the hand is most delicately drawn. The other

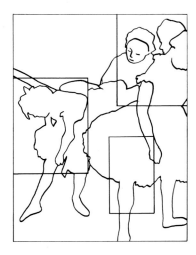

three heads are more finished.
The two observers, perhaps
mothers or friends, are
engaged in conversation and
are carefully delineated
although, interestingly and
typically, the most finished is
the one with the plumed hat
of whom least is seen. As
often happens in a closely knit
group when it is carefully
examined for the spatial
relationships, the scale and
position of this figure gives
rise to questions. Is there
enough room for her body between the dancer and the
wall? Is not her head too big?
And is the other not too
small? It is only when one
examines the work in this
realist, critical way that one
recognizes that the sense of
reality may actually be
artifice.

*This truly wonderful picture,
only measuring 63.4×48.2 cm
(25×19 in), shows its brilliance
in the top right-hand corner
(detail on previous page). Here
Degas has used different
techniques to solve his
problems. In order to bring out
the details of the old lady's
face he has done little more
than use pastel to highlight
her features, in contrast to the
economy of the rest of the
picture. Painting on a buff
background gave Degas the
opportunity to show his
eagerness and economy of style
(details this page). The two
techniques show his brilliance
in bringing each and every
part of the picture to life in
this very unusual composition.*

Ballet Dancer Taking a Bow
(*Danseuse au bouquet*)
1877 Pastel on paper
mounted on canvas
72 × 77.5cm (28⅜ × 30½in)
Musée d'Orsay
Paris

This pastel shows the full
stage with a dramatic
footlight illumination. It is
again a studio composition
and it is interesting to see
how this lighting effect is
achieved. It seems apparent
that the composition was
constructed with the principal
dancer in full light downstage
while the rest of the scene
was presented in somewhat

muted colour on a dark
coloured paper. The darker
area to the dancer's right
emphasizes her light tone. But
the effect of the footlights is
obtained almost exclusively by
the bottom lighting on the
head and shoulders and not on
the whole figure; indeed the
forward leg and foot are
hardly modelled at all and
there are no dramatically cast
shadows, as there would have
been on, say, the bouquet, the
tutu and the arms. The hand
and arm holding the tutu is
given a dark surround but the
effect of light is not treated as
it is on the head.

All this indicates studio

work where a retinal impression has been retained and is
superimposed on the scene
which is less dramatically
conceived. Indeed, the group of
figures on the left seems
almost in a differently lit
scene and the two dancers to
the left in orange and blue
are only cursorily – if deftly
– indicated. Nevertheless, the
sense of the whole ensemble is
precisely what it is supposed
to be and all the devices –
which are as clearly conceived
intellectually to achieve the
effect Degas wants as are the
means – are marvellously
controlled by a superb
technique.

The point of significance to
note here is how far in his
pictorial intention Degas is
from any Impressionist
precepts of light, colour and
visual interpretation. This is a
highly sophisticated scene
setting achieved by super-
lative technical manipulation.
The details to be examined in
this pastel are as revealing as
any that we could consider.

To make the point in
perhaps a more pungent
way, this is a highly un-
Impressionist impression.

*The detail right shows the
masterly understanding of
light on the subject.*

Ballet Dancers in the Wings
(*Danseuses derrière le portant*)
1900 Pastel on paper
71.1 × 66cm (28 × 26in)
St. Louis Art Museum
St. Louis
Missouri

The detail of this picture shows that Degas is the total master of his craft. He chooses his colours carefully, and his use of them shows his brilliance as a colourist.

In this late pastel there are indications of Degas' failing sight but nevertheless there are qualities of colour and draughtsmanship which reveal that he was still very much in intellectual and technical command of the pastel method. He had already all but abandoned oil painting for some years and pastel had become his usual method of painting. At this time he had also begun to make small sculptures of dancers and women in bathing poses. These were some of his most sensitive works and were designed partly to confirm information about form which he incorporated in his paintings. There are a number of sculptures and drawings in identical poses. Degas had a selection of favourite poses which he reused and which, as his sight deteriorated, became something of a stand-by. He was not alone in this practice of reusing poses; academics habitually reused poses that they considered effective and which had been praised by critics. Degas' reasons were not a search for popularity but a resort forced upon him in his later years when he could no longer see the actual events. It is a great tribute to his determination and dedication in most distressing circumstances.

His technique of necessity became broader, his drawing more schematic and his forms more simply expressed. At the same time his experience and knowledge offered opportunities of directness in drawing and colour which remind one of a late Titian.

Indeed, it is the pursuit of almost abstract qualities of colour/form relationships that concerns Degas most in many of his later works, including the one illustrated here. The lyrical quality of the unusual colour, ranging from yellows through greens to blues, is framed in notes of orange and brown on either edge, in the heads of the dancers. It might also be noted that there are deft touches of colour which indicate that his colour perception was unimpaired.

Café-Concert at the
Ambassadeurs
(*Le café-concert aux
Ambassadeurs*)
c.1876 – 7   Pastel on
monotype
37 × 27cm (14½ × 10⅝in)
Musée des Beaux-Arts
Lyons
France

*The picture illustrated right is
the original monotype. The
picture left, the reverse image
of the monotype, shows what
the original would have looked
like.*

*Details overleaf show the
broadness and simplicity of the
execution. Brushstrokes are
clearly visible from the
original.*

This small, densely peopled
pastel reflects the gay, even
riotous, evenings that nightly
took place at Les Ambassadeurs on the Champs-Elysées,
where groups of young men
dined, indiscriminately
applauded all the female
singers and launched
unwanted scraps of food onto
the stage. Degas, in his walks
along the streets of Paris,
would drop in to such
entertainments, and enjoyed
them as an observer. He made
a number of paintings of such
scenes and, although only a

small pastel, this is one of the
most effective.
   The work was included in
the third Impressionist
exhibition and was warmly
praised as conveying the full
atmosphere of the occasion.
These are essentially Parisian
entertainments and they
continued to produce powerful
singers and dancers until well
after Degas died, such as
Edith Piaf and Josephine
Baker.
   In considering this work it
has to be remembered that
working on a monotype base

reverses the original image
and that Degas, adopting his
usual practice of working his
composition up in his studio,
will have drawn the reverse
image of the one we see here.
It is often interesting and
instructive to look at such
monotype pastels in reverse –
through a mirror. In this
instance it is perhaps also
important. The painting seen
in reverse is a more familiar
form of Degas composition –
somewhat reminiscent of the
Orchestra Pit. The linear
aspects of the composition are,

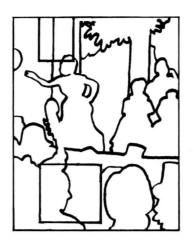

for example, much more evident.

What particularly distinguish this work are the oppositions within it, perhaps intended to reflect the strength and vitality of the occasion. Firstly, the low dark tones opposed to the extremely bright areas. The whole foreground action has been reduced in tonal range and detail to accommodate this, the only liveliness being found in the bonnets of the two girls in the audience. When this area is examined it will be noted that the spatial relationships in the foreground group are distorted and the scale of the figures is not consistent – the trumpet player appears to be wearing the bonnet! Nevertheless, the sense of crowded excitement of orchestra and audience is effectively evoked.

The high key area of the painting also includes the greatest colour oppositions; the blue dress and orange-yellow sash, the red dress and green colour notes surrounding it, provide the enhancement of complementaries making the top section a vibrant riot of romance, colour and light. The effect of the footlights is here expressed more consistently and effectively than in *Ballet Dancer Taking a Bow* (1877) but even so the tonal ranges are reduced for the sake of pictorial unity. As has been mentioned before, Degas is more concerned with the sensation of the scene – its impression – than with the visual literalness.

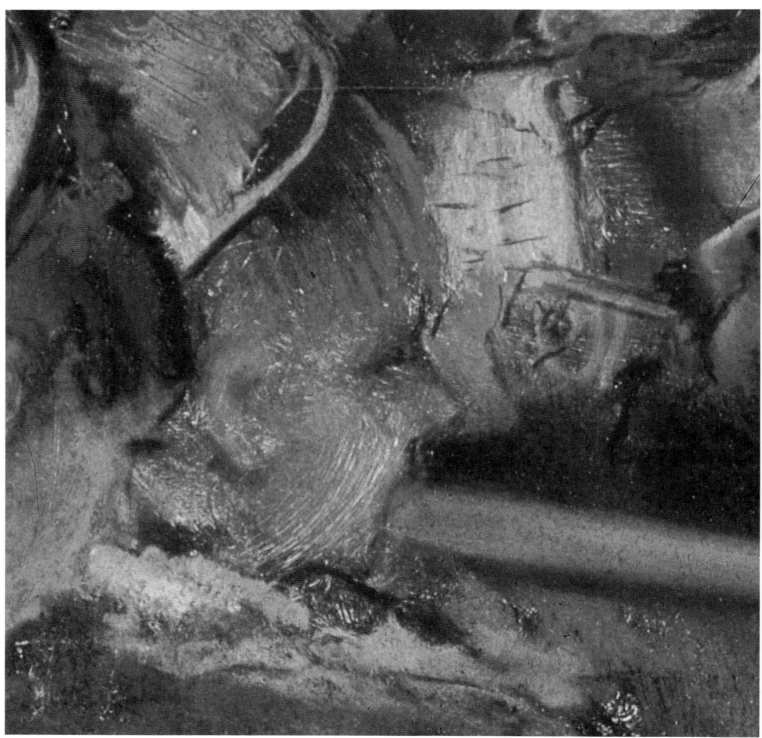

Reading the Letter
(*La lecture de la lettre*)
c.1882 Pastel on paper
63.5 × 45.7cm (25 × 18in)
Burrell Collection
Glasgow
Scotland

Lacking perhaps the glamour and popular appeal of his ballet dancers or his later studies of women bathing, but sandwiched between them in time, is a series of drawings and paintings of laundresses engaged in the various activities of their trade. When Degas was attracted to an area of subject matter he explored its possibilities as long as opportunity lasted and until he felt that he had, for him at least, exhausted its potential, as had happened with the horse and jockey theme.

He seems to have found the dark, unsavoury conditions, the unselfconscious working poses of the women, the cleanliness of the washed clothes and bed linen, and the bright coloured scarves etc. of the laundresses a visually fascinating subject. Here was a scene of significance in the great variety of Parisian life, as significant in its way as the ballet or the horserace. With the same disdain of social comment and the same keen observational eye as he had applied to the ballet or to jockeys and horses, he painted and drew laundresses at work and leisure.

For him they represented the world of labour and when this pastel was painted they had figured in two recently published books, Emile Zola's *L'Assommoir* (1878) and Joris Karl Huysmans' scenes of life, *Croquis Parisien* (1880).

Laundresses were then a very familiar part of the Parisian scene. Paris was so highly regarded as a laundry centre that washing was even sent from England. Most of the clean and soiled linen was carried by hand through the streets by the laundresses and they were a common, affectionately accepted group with their large baskets on their hips.

When Edmond de Goncourt, a celebrated literary figure and novelist, visited Degas' studio in 1874 he observed that the 'rose of the flesh in the white of the linen, in the milky mist of the gauze [was] the most delightful excuse for light and tender colour'. Degas' paintings of laundresses made observers, unfamiliar with the 'lower classes' and the actual work conditions of the laundresses, understand how they felt, looked and spoke as well as how they used an iron, folded clothes and carried them. This was information as objectively dispensed and with as little social comment as were the visions of the ballet.

In the pastel *Reading the Letter* the scene tells a story – or seems to although the message is not clear. Evidently the letter is being read aloud and it may be that the recipient is not the reader but the girl leaning over the table and gazing in concentration at nothing while absorbing the message.

At all events, Degas is here probably reconstructing a scene that he had witnessed without himself necessarily understanding its importance to the participants. To him, however, the relationships of light and dark, of colour and line, would have constituted the principal interest.

In the oil painting *Two Laundresses* from about 1884, Degas has again taken a scene which tells a story, this time with more obvious social observation. The figure on the left is painted with more than usual finish and with the usual assured draughtsmanship. All the tired boredom and the 'low life' suggestive of a Dutch 17th century genre painting by Breuwer or Van Ostade are encapsulated in this figure, but with a freshness and immediacy that removes all suggestion of acute deprivation that is immanent in their work.

The detail of the head, left, clearly shows with just a few strokes of pastel how Degas captured the mood of the subject.

At the Milliner's
(*Chez la modiste*)
c.1883 Pastel on paper
76 × 85cm (30 × 30½ in)
Thyssen-Bornemisza Collection
Lugano
Switzerland

In this elaborate and more
than usually worked pastel,
Degas has treated another
subject of Parisian life which
engaged his interest at the
same time as he was working
on the laundress theme. He
painted a number of scenes
inside a milliner's shop while
young girls attended by
friends and salesladies are
trying on or examining hats;
around them are other models.
The subject is a far cry from

the deprived and simple
interiors of the laundry. Here
all is colour and pattern, style
and elegance.
   All the qualities of Degas'
draughtsmanship are brought
to bear in this work as well as
his love for striking colour
effects and combinations. He
has also made much of the
surface textures of fabrics and
straw hats, their weave
patterns and the softness of
silks and satins. This is a
luxury world and Degas has
given it a full sense of
leisured privilege. Degas' own
rich decorative sense is given
full rein. The drawing of the
figure in black is particularly
acute and highly finished
while the delicacy of the

drawing of her gloved hand is
a vivid and exciting reminder
of Degas' skill. The colour
harmonies and contrasts are
of such a range as to
constitute a controlled colour
symphony not found elsewhere
in his work. The bonnet at the
top left of the painting is an
inspired note of cool elegance
and tonal attack which is the
key to the sense of warmth of
the whole work, and balances
the figure in black without
competing with it.
   Such painting offers a visual
seductiveness that awakens
awe and envy of the
sensitivity of genius. It would
require only this work to
establish Degas as a great
painter. The subtleties are so

numerous that the work will
repay almost endless study.
   In the *Café-Concert at the
Ambassadeurs* we have noted
Degas thrusting the fore-
ground figures into an
unnatural, impossible spatial
relationship. Although less
compacted, the same is, to a
degree, true of this work. It is
difficult, if not impossible, to
determine where the lower
part of the friend (mother?) in
brown is located in relation to
the young girl in black; the
latter, being drawn with much
greater definition, tends to
advance towards the picture
plane. The pushing of the
action towards the picture
plane is used extensively by
Degas and he adopts various

devices to achieve this. Other painters whose intention was similar to Degas' — as, for instance Caravaggio in his *Supper at Emmaus* (National Gallery, London) or *Conversion of Saul* (Sta. Maria del Popolo, Rome) — made use of the same effect and for the same reasons. Degas wanted the observer to be a participant in the scene, to feel involved in the action, and thus drew him towards the subject and thrust the elements of the painting towards the observer.

Part of the method used by Degas was to adopt a steep, curved perspective which places the observer looking down on the subject. In this case the observer first looks down on the table and the hats, and then upwards towards the figure in black, noting, as the glance passes, the figure in brown. But since the attraction and interest lies in the young girl trying on the hat, she is carefully delineated, while the figure in brown is more broadly drawn. She is also diminished in perception by the black bonnet on the left, providing a note which quickly leads to the other black element, the girl in the hat. Opulent is the word for this pastel.

Details left and below reveal the insight of Degas' mind regarding colour and form. The drawing in this picture is almost irrelevant. The shapes and colours join forces in one harmonious composition.

Women Before a Café: Evening
(*Femmes devant un café,
le soir*)
1877   Pastel on monotype
41 × 60cm (16⅛ × 23⅝in)
Cabinet des Dessins
Musée du Louvre
Paris

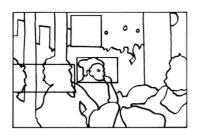

A further Parisian theme in Degas' work is found in his café scenes. Then as now the café was the centre of social life at all levels. We have noted that such places as the Café Guerbois and the Nouvelle Athènes were literary and artistic meeting places. Similar cafés, less famous, catered for the workers, professional men and even for prostitutes. Each café had its own character and a clientele that fitted in with it and helped to form it. Most had some tables on the street in front, where customers could see and be seen. Mirrors, decorated columns, posters, pendant lights, bottles and glasses, chairs and tables gave café life a visually varied and colourful attraction, and were a frequent subject for many painters.

Degas himself liked to stroll the streets at night — he claimed with probable justice that the sunlight hurt his

The details of this painting show the mastery of technique: the broadness of the pastel strokes are the same in the detail as in the background. This is the work of an artist who is in complete command of his idiom.

eyes – and particularly loved Montmartre where, on the Boulevard Montmartre, the café in this pastel was located.

A typical café scene is depicted on a monotype base. Seen from inside the café with the street and the distant shops in the background, young girls, evidently prospecting prostitutes, are sipping drinks. They are not physically very appealing; only the central figure manages to appear at all provocative, but Degas has chosen to show her flicking her teeth with her thumb in a common gesture.

The composition is daring and original. Using the vertical column division which he had used elsewhere (see page 69, *Jockeys Before the Race*), he has created a spatial box which focuses the interest on the seated figures, giving them an architectural context. Opposed to the firm verticals are the arabesques of the chair backs and the line of the figures forming a sweeping S curve in opposition to the verticals. It is also worth noting another familiar device of Degas': the figures on the extreme right and left are cut off at the edge of the painting. This has the effect of indicating that the action continues outside the picture, that it is a slice of life only; also the figures at the edges focus attention on the beautifully drawn central figure.

Woman Getting out of her Bath
(*Femme sortant du bain*)
1877 Pastel on monotype
23 × 31cm (9 × 12¼ in)
Cabinet des Dessins
Musée du Louvre
Paris

This small monotype reversed pastel is a charming, intimate example of Degas' last major subject – women bathing, washing, drying, combing their hair and those other private and personal activities that are necessary in preparing for the day – or for the bed. They represent a special category of Degas' work and in this and the following three examples we shall consider the various aspects of this part of his *oeuvre*.

Because of its small dimensions, this work has been reproduced here at nearly full size. One of the usual difficulties that writers and publishers of books on art always have – not of course entirely avoidable and not avoided elsewhere in this book – is to give a sense of the actual scale of a work of art. When the image is reduced to fit into a page it is concentrated in a way that may be misleading, and it is worth considering the dimensions, which are usually printed with the description, when studying any reproduction.

Although Degas never married he had a lifelong interest in women. He had many women friends and, as we have already seen, women are the most frequent subjects in his work. Indeed, apart from the early historical paintings and the horse and jockey series, most of his subjects have included women as an important element, most frequently the most important. It would not be true to say that he held them generally in the highest intellectual esteem but he was most certainly attracted to them. There seems no foundation in the suggestions, probably based only on the fact that he never married, that he was either a misogynist or a homosexual.

There is a further charge sometimes laid against him that he was a voyeur. Perhaps he is himself partly responsible for this since George Moore reports Degas as saying, apropos a pastel

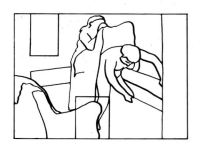

Form must be defined so that the image left little to the imagination or to interpretation. For the Impressionist and for Degas, suggestion and implication carried important messages. When Degas submitted work which showed changes of intention not disguised, areas unresolved, colour floating and independent of form, the works were first seen as studies, unfinished or abandoned. Since that time we have developed an interest in seeing the processes of creation, recognizing that they will usually expand the perceptions and understanding of the observer. Degas' part in this, through such works as are illustrated here, should not be underestimated.

such as this, that he saw his models as if through a keyhole. Of course, the essential element in voyeurism is visual sexual stimulation accompanying the secret viewing of naked bodies or sexual activity. But there is no evidence from his paintings of Degas being a voyeur. Indeed, any examination of the paintings themselves will indicate that although the women are seen in private activity there is such sympathy without salacity in Degas' treatment of them that, even were the charge true, it could not be based on these deeply human studies.

They are, nevertheless, different and in some senses revolutionary. The acceptable nude in 19th century French art, as Manet had found to his cost, carried 'classical' overtones and was a desexualized figure of marble impersonality usually depicting a remote historical or mythological subject. A sense of actuality, of flesh and blood, of a contemporary naked figure was unacceptable. Perfect form, devoid of imperfections inherent in the individual, was sought by the academics and their critics. Heavy, experienced bodies engaged in mundane activities might be useful as learning studies but they were definitely not the stuff of high art.

It is a measure of the patent distinction of Degas' work that he was not only able to exhibit these paintings and receive critical approval but that he revolutionized the public appreciation of the body as a 'modern' subject. Of course he was not alone in trying to widen acceptable subject matter and the public's appreciation of it, and to this extent he is part of the Impressionist as well as the Independent movement.

Another academic concern was with 'finish'. It was, the academics believed, the painter's responsibility to resolve all the pictorial problems the subject presented.

The broadness of the brushstrokes has been enhanced by the pastel painting on the monotype to make this picture tonally perfect (see details below). It is worth noting that the painting as reproduced in this book is larger than actual size.

The Tub
1886   Pastel on paper
60 × 83cm (23⅝ × 32⅝in)
Musée d'Orsay
Paris

103

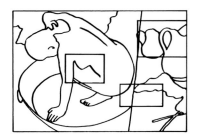

The details here show the mastery that Degas had over pastel. In some instances he used a steady technique of horizontal or vertical hatching, the intensity of which brings out form and softness, such as the model's hip. On the other hand, he would discard all technique and flamboyantly chisel out details such as the jug below. Nevertheless, the different techniques combine to make a unified composition.

Degas' reported comment that he saw his subjects as if through a keyhole gives a further indication of the poses in which his bathers are drawn. Unselfconsciously carrying out their ablutions, imagining themselves un-observed, they provided Degas with unusual opportunities for pose and composition. In the two *Tub* pastels illustrated on pages 102 and 106, using the same model he makes the hard metallic circular form of the tub itself a foil to the soft forms of the model's back. Here again he has, in both instances, adopted a steep perspective which places the observer — and painter — in close, intimate proximity to the scene. It is not so much a key-hole as a fly-on-the-wall view.

These are both well worked up pastels of great compositional invention. They are not the casual study done from life, and from what has already been said of Degas' working practices it will be

understood that he made numerous studies before finished work. These studies were done in a variety of methods from charcoal black and white drawings, sometimes heightened with a little colour, to oil and essence sketches, and including pastel. Degas did not regard oil painting as the inevitable, natural method for a finished work as we know that most of the works illustrated here were exhibited by him in mixed exhibitions. This view of oil paint, it may also be noted, was not that of the academics, for whom oil painting was the exhibition method, or generally that of the Impressionists, although some of them did work in pastel. Degas' natural curiosity and independence led him to use many different methods and combinations, and as long as the result was what he wanted he regarded the subject as fit for showing.

It is difficult, seeing these

beautiful, sensitive, sympathetic works, not to believe in Degas' great care for women; his caressing vision of these unusual poses reveals a caring portrayal of a felt relationship.

In both pastels the careful cross-hatch technique and marvellous control of tone and surface texture are fully displayed. The solidity and authority of, for instance, the arm and hand holding the sponge (Hill-Stead) or the hand pressed in the tub (d'Orsay) are examples of Degas' refined draughtsmanship. In both instances the dense drawing of the back exhibits his deep knowledge of human anatomy, acquired through lifelong study.

These two pastels show Degas at the height of his power. They also confirm what George Moore had perceptively noted — that Degas' nudes broke new ground and were astonishingly innovative.

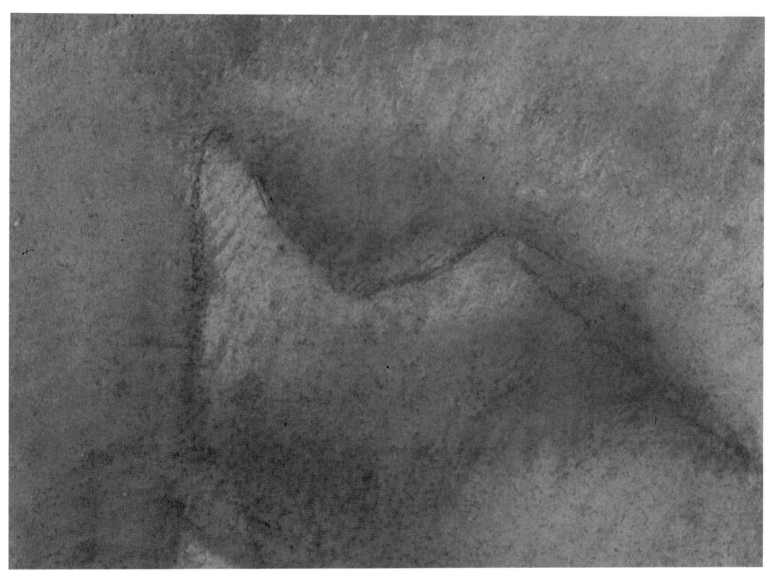

The Tub
1886 Pastel on paper
70 × 70cm (27½ × 27½ in)
Hill-Stead Museum
Farmington
Connecticut

*The details shown here
illustrate the simplicity of tone
(detail opposite top) and the
sculptural quality (detail
opposite below) which contribute to the draughtsmanlike
quality of this picture.*

*Woman at her Toilet
(Woman Drying Herself)
(Aprés le bain, femme
s'essuyant)*
c.1895 – 1905
Pastel on tissue mounted
on board
69.7 × 72.4cm (27½ × 28½in)
Art Institute
Chicago
Illinois

*The details opposite show the
surface quality of a Degas
pastel. Every stroke of the
pastel brings the surface
quality of the material to life.*

This late work, when Degas' vision was undoubtedly severely restricted, is extraordinary for its bold, coarse strength, brilliant and violent colour, and dense surface working. Lacking some of the refinement of detail of earlier work, the forms are boldly drawn.

Resulting from the numerous drawings that he made of each pose, and created with the assurance of experience, this work is a late masterpiece comparable in the opulence of composition and colour with the earlier *At the Milliner's* (page 92).

The work is composed of four sheets of tracing paper glued to a sulphite board — another example of Degas' experimental seeking for a precise effect.

The colour, in its intensity, seems to relate more to the Expressionist work of this century than to Impressionism or Post Impressionism, although there is some small echo of Gauguin in the emotional impact that the work has.

The pastel is heavily worked — sometimes several layers thick — with something of the undercolour showing through and increasing the colour intensities. Charcoal has been used to outline the forms and has been subsequently worked over.

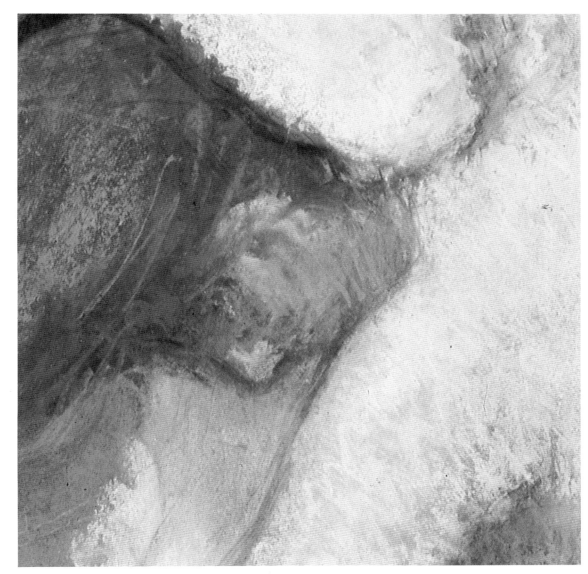

Two Dancers Resting
(*Deux danseuses au repos*)
c.1910 Pastel on paper
78 × 96cm (30¾ × 37¾in)
Musée d'Orsay
Paris

The vertical strokes of the pastel to execute the figures, as shown in the detail opposite top, are nothing more than a shorthand to bring this harmonious picture to a conclusion.

In this very late work, appropriately enough a pastel of ballet dancers, Degas' working method at this time in the building up of his figures from a simplified naked form is evident in both dancers. They are drawn so that their clothes are almost transparent and the composition is more an abstract linear arabesque than a study of the dancers and their costumes. Adjustments to the form are left and the simplifications and corrections to the figure on the left show his attempts not so much to achieve an accurate rendering of a pose but to make the figure fit within a compositional intention. Degas is here exploring near abstract relationships of interlocked line and form in a way that relates him more to 20th century experiments than to anything that could be thought of as Impressionist. Indeed, it should be remembered that Fauvism as a movement was over and Cubism was the avant garde rage in Paris when this work was completed.

The delicacy of the colour in this work contrasts strongly with the violence of attack in the colour of the previous pastel. It is as if, lacking clear vision, he is expressing experience and sensation in an arrangement of forms. It still incorporates much of Degas' compositional inventiveness but the acute authority of the earlier drawing is replaced by a mellow simplicity.

*Woman Seated on a Balcony,
New Orleans*
(*Femme assise sur un balcon,
Nouvelle-Orléans*)
(Estelle Musson?)
1872–3 Pastel on paper
64 × 77cm (25¼ × 30¼ in)
Ordrupgaard Museum
Copenhagen

Degas' stay with the Musson family in New Orleans was an experience that he much enjoyed although he decided not to paint the local scene since, as he stated, Paris and Louisiana would not mix. He regarded the period spent there as one of reflection and intellectual and spiritual recuperation. He enjoyed the bustling life of New Orleans, the colour and the scenery, but most of all he enjoyed the family life.

Estelle Musson was married to his brother René and he was very fond of her. He had a special sympathy with her since shortly before her marriage she had gone blind. She was a very sympathetic character and Degas, in a letter to his friend, the bassoonist Dihau, wrote that Estelle bore her blindness in an incomparable manner so that she needed little help about the house and scarcely ever bumped into furniture, having memorized all the positions.

Although there is no certain attribution of this pastel as a portrait of Estelle there are certain similarities which suggest it might be. If not it was another member of the numerous family household seated on the first floor balcony of the home.

The composition is unfinished — the balcony barely sketched in with ruled lines, and the hands holding an object which may be a bag or a fan — but the portrait itself is most delicately drawn with Degas' own special sense of colour. His use of ribbons, edging, sashes and hats to add a determining note of colour which enlivens and pulls together the composition, is familiar in his work. Here the golden yellow trimming and the black neckband have this effect.

It is an example of Degas' portraiture. In the 1860s and 1870s he painted a number of distinguished portraits, most of them in oils although preliminary pencil, charcoal or pastel sketches always preceded them. In these his great abilities as a draughtsman were always evident. They carry a conviction of likeness, not only in a physical, visual sense but in a quality of character. It is one of the many indications that, despite a fastidious aloofness, there was a deep human warmth in his nature.

113

The details shown in these enlargements reveal just how important the background is as a complement to the main subject.

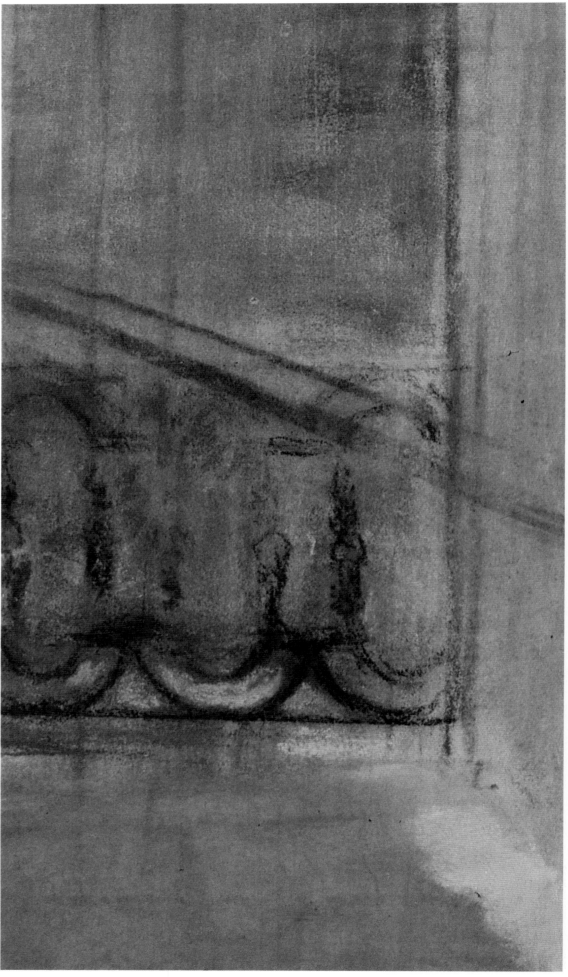

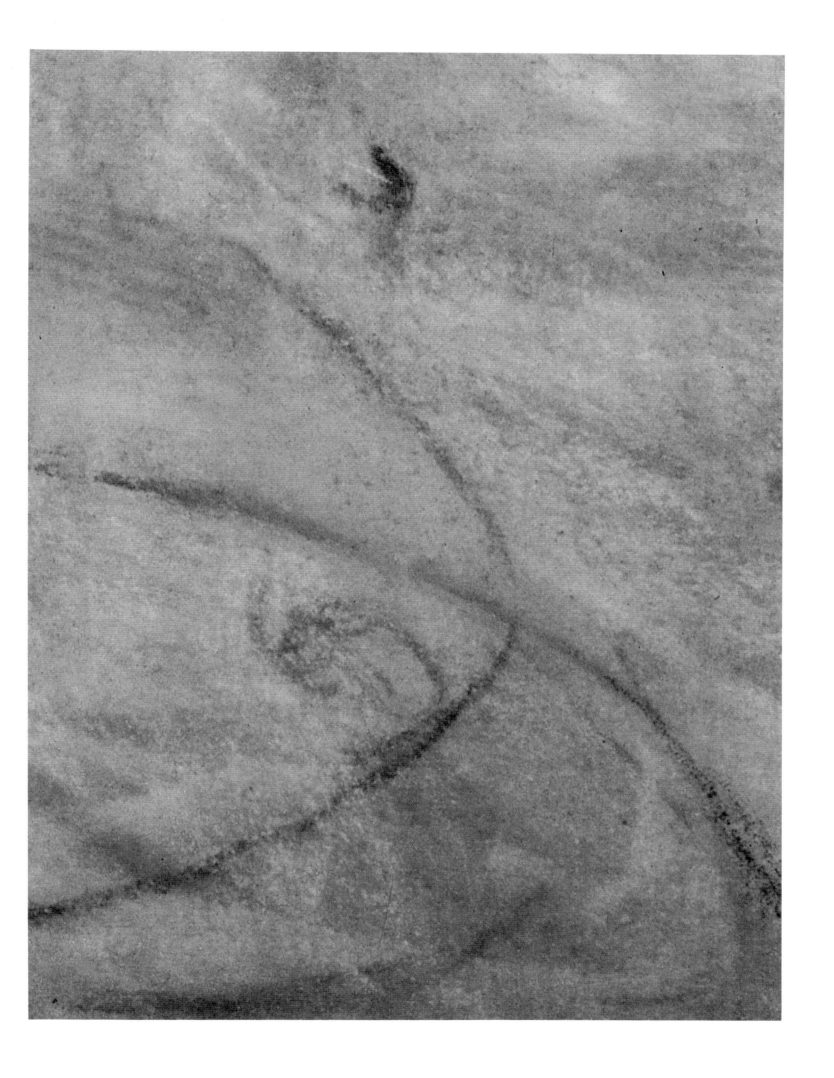

Mlle. Malo
c.1877 Pastel on paper
52 × 41cm (20½ × 16⅛in)
Barber Institute of Fine Arts
University of Birmingham
England

The failure of the family bank in 1874, after the death of Degas' father, had left the painter in financial difficulties and he had to move to less expensive accommodation. Around this time two further embarrassing scandals surrounded him. His brother René left his blind wife Estelle in 1878, causing a rift between René and Edgar which lasted many years.

The second scandal which also occurred around this time concerned his brother Achille who was attacked on the steps of the Paris Bourse by a M. Legrand and who, in turn, drew a revolver and shot his assailant, wounding him. Achille was arrested and sentenced to six months in prison.

The reason for the affray was that Mme. Legrand was a former dancer and mistress of Achille who had borne him a son who had died. Mme. Legrand's stage name was Thérèse Mallot and there is a strong possibility amounting to a probability that this pastel is a portrait of her; there are four portraits of her and they may have been done when Achille was still seeing her — after her marriage. The whole appalling episode must have been extremely distasteful to Degas' patrician spirit.

Thérèse Mallot was known as an attractive woman and Degas has presented her in this fine pastel in a sympathetic light. Although a simple, straightforward study, the variety of Degas' handling of the pastel medium in the sketch is, as usual, masterly.

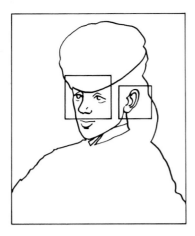

By using diagonal pastel strokes, Degas has employed the technique to enhance the flesh tones of the face and the ear, shown on the previous page and below.

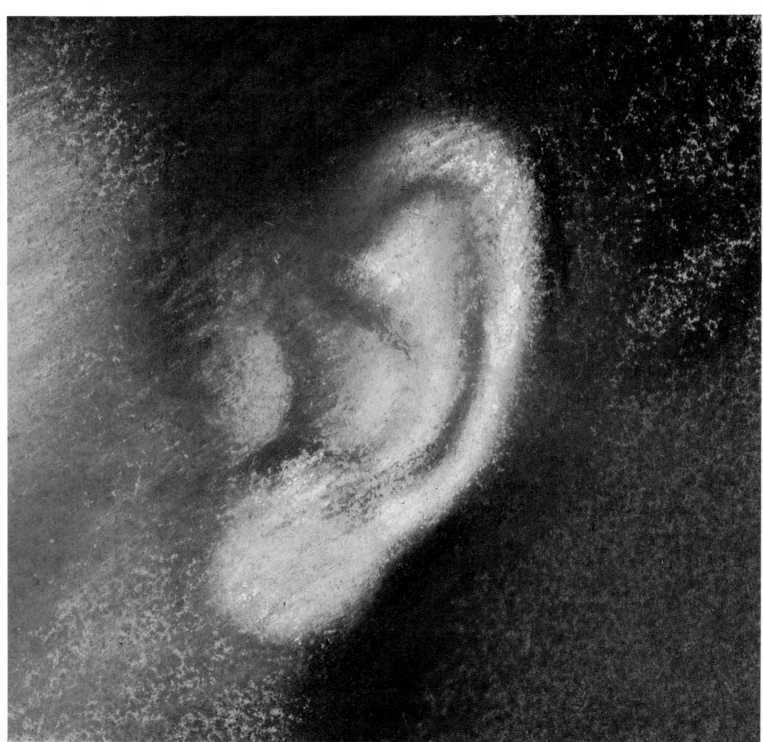

INDEX

Figures in italics refer to illustrations

Photographic acknowledgments

© 1990 The Art Institute of Chicago, Illinois, Mr and Mrs Martin A Ryerson Collection. All rights reserved. 108, 109 top, 109 bottom; Barber Institute of Fine Arts, The University of Birmingham 68, 69 top, 69 bottom, 116, 117, 118; Bridgeman Art Library, London 2, 4–5, 9, 36–37, 86, 87, 88, 89, cover; The Burrell Collection, Glasgow Museums and Art Galleries 58, 59 top, 59 bottom, 64–65, 66, 67, 74–75, 76 top, 76 bottom, 77, 90, 91; Sterling and Francine Clark Art Institute, Williamstown, Massachusetts 6; Denver Art Museum, Colorado 78, 79, 80, 81; Mary Evans Picture Library, London 19, 44–45; Photographie Giraudon, Paris 7, 10–11, 14–15, 20, 32–33, 34–35, 46–47, 50–51, 51 top, 94–95, 96 top, 96 bottom, 97, 102–103, 104, 105 top, 105 bottom; Hill-Stead Museum, Farmington, Connecticut 106, 107 top, 107 bottom; Mansell Collection, London 40, 42, 43; Mr and Mrs Paul Mellon, Upperville, Virginia 13; Metropolitan Museum of Art, New York 8; Musées Nationaux, Paris 12, 52–53, 54–55, 56 top, 56 bottom, 57 top, 57 bottom, 60–61, 62 top, 62 bottom, 63, 82, 83, 98–99, 100, 101, 110, 111 top, 111 bottom; National Gallery, London 30, 31 top, 31 bottom, 41; Ordrupgaardsamlingen, Charlottenlund 48, 49, 112, 113, 114, 115; Sammlung Oskar Reinhart "Am Römerholz", Winterthur 38–39; St Louis Art Museum, Missouri 84, 85; Tate Gallery, London 16, 17; Thyssen-Bornemisza Collection, Lugano 70–71, 72, 73 top, 73 bottom, 92, 93 top, 93 bottom; Windsor Castle, Royal Library © 1990 Her Majesty the Queen 29 right.

Front cover:	(main picture and top details) *Café-Concert at the Ambassadeurs.* c. 1876–7. Musée des Beaux-Arts, Lyons (bottom left) *The Tub* (detail). 1886. Musée d'Orsay, Paris (bottom right) *Women Before a Café: Evening* (detail). 1877. Musée du Louvre, Paris
Back cover:	*Miss Lala at the Cirque Fernando.* 1879. Tate Gallery, London.
Title spread:	*Woman Combing Her Hair.* Musée du Louvre, Paris.
Contents spread:	*Woman Drying Herself.* National Gallery of Scotland, Edinburgh

Illustrations by Trewin Copplestone 22, 23 top, 23 bottom, 24, 25, 26–27, 27 top, 27 bottom, 28, 29 left.